THE GOLDEN PATH

CHANNELED BY

RUTH RYDEN

THE GOLDEN PATH

An Introduction to Advanced Spiritual Knowledge

By Higher-Dimensional Master Teachers Peter, Sananda, Hilarian, Kathumi, William and Marian, who currently combine their thoughts to be known as the Beings of Light.

The Christ Spirit is often part of this group when teachings are sent for the *Children of Light Newsletter,* self-published by the channel, and for other publications.

Channeled by Ruth Ryden

Cover art by
Richard Van der Heijden

ISBN 929385-43-8

Published by
Light Technology Publishing
P.O. Box 1526
Sedona, AZ 86339

Printed by
Mission Possible Commercial Printing
P.O. Box 1495
Sedona, AZ 86339

Dedication

Far in the future of your planet
There are states of mind to be acquired,
Abilities and bodies of Light
That open the gates of higher dimensions
to mankind.
It is to this higher potential
That this book of lessons is dedicated.

PETER

Table of Contents

Foreword by the Channel
Description of Spiritual Teachers

PART ONE:
BASIC CONCEPTS EXPLAINED

PART TWO:
BIBLE STORIES REVISITED

Foreword

My sincere thanks and blessings to you for acquiring this book and reading it. The Blessed Masters who have sent these words through me directed the time that the lessons were to be published and the time is now. If this way of thinking is new to you, give yourself time to think about each concept that is different from your present way of thinking. If there is something you cannot accept at this stage of your study, let it be. Later on, you may see it differently. Everyone progresses at his or her own speed.

The lessons in this book were given over a period of three years and I came to understand that they were given clearly, concisely and lovingly for those who are just opening their minds and hearts to the truths that have not been available to them before. It was hard for me when I had difficulty finding a publisher right away because the lessons are of such power and beauty. But I was directed to be patient; when the time was right the publisher would come to me. And so she did.

My personal background is that of wife, mother and grandmother. I worked as a legal secretary for 20 years, which was obviously training for this inspired writing. After working with automatic writing for some time, the words and thoughts started coming through my mind in the form of inspired writing. In 1980 to 1983, teachings began to appear from my Master Teacher Peter. From then on, I knew what my lifetime path would be.

I have worked with many people over the years, giving spiritual counseling and teaching by contacting each individual's personal spiritual teachers and receiving the needed information and guidance. This has been most rewarding and I am now able to do this by mail, also.

Trance channeling is still in the future for me, I believe, and I have given the Masters permission to use me in this manner when the time is right.

At the time of publication of this book, I am self-publishing the monthly *Children of Light Newsletter*, which is entirely channeled material dealing with present problems, future anticipations, predictions of weather and Earth changes and spiritual lessons.

You may contact me:

Mrs. Ruth Ryden
HCR Box 313
Whispering Pines
Payson, AZ 85541
(602) 474-3515

Teachers who have channeled information for this book as they describe themselves

MASTER TEACHER PETER

Peter is but an essence of the ancient soul who once incarnated as one of the disciples of Jesus, the Christ, during His sojourn on Earth and who speaks to you now from the sixth dimension. This soul is one of the spiritual Hierarchy created by the Most High to do His works and to care for His children on the Planet Earth. Peter is only one of many souls who have been given the commission of teaching those incarnated as human beings the knowledge your generation needs now during the last years of the present age. Take heed of them; learn and use what is important to you. The knowledge of the universe is so overpowering, even to the Hierarchy, that only a soul that has progressed to higher powers can possibly understand even a portion of it. We can only transmit to the best of our ability what can be understood and used by you. We send you our blessings and ask for yours.

MASTER TEACHER SANANDA

This soul had the most blessed honor to incarnate as the child Jesus two millennia ago. After the death on the cross, my spiritual essence, or being, returned to the sixth dimension where I reside. In the past ten years or so of your time, I have been instrumental in preparing and disseminating knowledge throughout your solar system about the wonderful changes occurring all through your universe and on the Planet Earth. Many spiritual beings from the sixth dimension are sending small parts of themselves that you term essences to humanity to instruct those who are able to hear and be aware of our presence. We are also instructing many other-world beings who have taken on the responsibility of remaining near you in order to help and instruct when possible. There are many fifth-dimensional beings who are being instructed by the Hierarchy to work with human minds to prepare you for the massive increase in your vibrational frequencies. Humanity is evolving into creatures of extremely high spiritual knowledge and your bodies will also evolve into a lighter consistency. All of this is what we are endeavoring to bring to you through many devoted channels all over the world. My work in the Hierarchy is with all created souls, surrounding them with love, peace and the all-pervasive knowledge of all universes. God Bless You All.

MASTER TEACHER HILARIAN

I am a member of the Hierarchy who has spent several lifetimes on your planet for many·reasons. I have been rulers and peasants, those of evil intent and those of high ideals. Thousands of years and lifetimes of learning have given this soul being the right to work closely with the Christ Spirit and others who have attained the same mastery. I dwell in the sixth dimension and my eternal work now is with evolving souls and evolving social relationships on your planet. I oversee many of the other-world beings who are now close to you and are also trying to ease your way into the new age of spiritual knowledge. I send words of knowledge through many channels of your world so that the knowledge may be seen and heard by as many people as possible. Time is growing short. Read, study and accept what you know in your inner heart to be true. On the spiritual level that you will eventually return to, this is already known; you just need to have your memory jogged a bit. I shall be pleased if you will listen and I bless you whether you do or not.

MASTER TEACHER KATHUMI

The spelling of my name that you are using is correct. The Kuthumi of tradition who is an Ascended Master is only one part of my created soul who has served mankind for hundreds of years and is still doing so. The essence that you are communicating with is separate and distinct from Kuthumi; that is the reason for the different spelling of the name. There have been very few times when I have communicated with those in matter and would not have done so at this time, except that this is a time, the end of an era, when many of us in the Hierarchy are sending out strong messages in the clearest manner possible. I reside in the sixth dimension and have never embodied into human form. I am a soul created by the Almighty One to act in a supervisory position, being one of the regulators of the energies of all created planets and of their inhabitants. Therefore, most of the teachings I will be sending through you will be regarding energy in some form or another.

MASTER TEACHER WILLIAM

My name, at least for you to recognize me by, will be William. Since there has never been a time when my vibrations have incarnated into a human body, I really have no human name. In this sixth dimension, we are known to one another by our personal vibratory rates, and that is more than sufficient.

It is my purpose at this time to transmit information that will help those of you who are teaching the Word of God to others to see more clearly the Creator's plan for your planet and for the universe in these last years of an age. We realize that the human mind is finite and cannot possibly grasp more than a portion of the infinite knowledge that the Creator has given into the ethers of time, but there is much more that can be learned and taught at your level of understanding that should now be heard.

It is my pleasure to be allowed to assist in this manner.

MASTER TEACHER MARIAN

You may refer to me as a "she," since my essence leans toward the feminine aspect. I dwell in the sixth dimension and venture out of it only seldom. My work in the Hierarchy is comprised of working with the many spirit essences who have spent lifetimes in your world and others who have returned before reaching childhood and supervising those teachers who bring them back to their full knowledge as eternal beings. I feel it necessary to send the lesson on how to activate the third eye as a teaching tool for humanity to regain lost knowledge. When there is further need of this kind, I will speak through this channel again. Our special blessings upon those of you who are working so hard to accomplish this for yourselves and others.

PART ONE

BASIC CONCEPTS EXPLAINED

CHAPTER ONE

The Process of Channeling

By Master Teacher Peter

This channel asked Peter to explain, as clearly as possible, the process by which an entity or soul not incarnated in a human body communicates information to the conscious mind of a human being. Also, what amount, if any, of this information originates from the higher self of the human personality? These questions are surely in the minds of most of you who have decided to read this book to further your knowledge of spiritual matters. The following lesson is his answer.

First of all, souls who have attained superior knowedge in the far reaches of time and space and who transmit information to those embodied on the Earth plane are usually commissioned to do so by either the Most High or the Christ Spirit. It is not something just anyone in spirit can take a notion to do. It requires that the entity reconstruct, so to speak, its vibrational patterns in order to be able to match the vibrations of the chosen channel in the third dimension. A soul who has progressed to a very high vibrational pattern is able to transmit knowledge learned over centuries, information directed to be given by the Holy Ones, and teachings that are appropriate for individuals or for humanity as a whole. When the vibrational patterns are lowered, the work that the high soul is doing on its own level has to be put aside for a time. Even if only a small essence of that soul has lowered its vibrational pattern, this is so to a large extent. Therefore, in order that the "computer" not be shut down in the eternal machinery of the universe, only a selected few are commissioned to perform this service to mankind.

There are many entities on the lower planes of existence who are also able to channel to people who believe they are receiving something wonderful. But remember, an entity who has just crossed over the boundary line between Earthly life and eternity has not changed its vibrations to a great degree and finds it very easy to communicate to a human mind that is open to its pattern. There are pitfalls when this kind of channeling is so prevalent. There are dark forces who push forward in a person's mind in order to give false or misleading information. There are also Earth-bound souls (who have chosen not to ascend back into the higher dimensions for many reasons) who wish to confuse, mislead or merely to channel some writing or verbal information to satisfy their still-active egos.

Those who wish to open themselves to be a channel can do so by careful assessment of their own priorities, the need to serve God in that manner, and by meditative techniques that lead to an open mind or channel. Sometimes only one or two of these criteria are met, and the person receives material only from an entity who has crossed over and wishes to communicate. Most of the time this is done in good faith and with the best of intentions. The newly returned spirit is able to see many things more clearly and wishes to help those left behind. This provides some interesting sessions, but not much real knowledge of the spiritual world.

Indian guides are a good example of this. The American Indian people have always been a highly spiritual race and feel obligated to help humanity when they return to Spirit. Some of them do a great deal of good with their communications, often reaching higher to find for their listeners deeper information that they had no previous knowledge of. We do not condemn this practice, but wish you to be aware that knowledge — universal knowledge — is vital for humanity to receive at this time. This knowledge can be acquired only from those in the fifth dimension or higher. If teachers admit that they are only in the fourth dimension (and they must, if asked), know that their discourses will be limited to their own knowledge and what they can observe at that level.

When a soul, or entity, from the higher dimensions is commissioned to transmit universal knowledge to humanity, the search begins for a human personality who will be able to pass on this information to others, who has accomplished a clear mind to act as a channel, who is willing to spend considerable amounts of time with the project, and whose personal vibrations are similar enough to the teacher's to be able to touch in unity for the time period involved in the channeling sessions. There are times when extremely important transmissions are sent to personalities who have no idea at first of what is going on. This has been done so that the material will not have any competition from the mind of the channel. The chosen channel in such cases often is most unhappy and confused about the whole thing, but the material still comes through undamaged. At the channel's soul level, this was a purpose of their lives, although at the conscious level, a big surprise. Only with the permission of the soulself is this ever done.

Depending upon the channel involved, knowledge is sent in several different ways. During the centuries, a human personality has received inspired communications mostly from voices in his or her mind, now termed clairaudience. This is still done and many human personalities are beginning to open their minds and listen for such communication. Many who are able to do so share this kind of communication with others, sometimes as a business, giving "readings." Again, fourth-dimensional beings find it easy to communicate in this manner. Most readings are given from this level. Those who open their minds to this kind of communication too easily find it very difficult to turn the voices off and it becomes a constant chattering.

At a more intensive level, higher-dimensional teachers go much deeper into the mind of the channel to implant knowledge by merging with his/her conscious thoughts, sometimes giving an entire concept to the channel's mind to be changed into words that express the concept clearly. Sometimes the merging is done by dictating the material through the language of the channel, using the channel's knowledge of the language to interpret what needs to be said. (That is the case with this present channel.) When the channel gets too interested and unconsciously begins to add his or her own thoughts, the flow of information is stopped until the channel realizes what is happening. This method is called "automatic writing" by humanity, although that is not entirely correct. Automatic writing is a method by which the sender takes control of the arm and hand of the channel and writes the information without the conscious knowledge of the channel. This is not used by higher entities because it bypasses the mind and will use that person without permission. Information given this way is often given by the dark forces, by those who wish to transmit their own views, regardless of the will of the channel, or by those who try to control the unwilling channel in some way. Any communication by Master Teachers commissioned by the Holy Ones is given through and with the permission of the soulself of the human channel. "Inspired writing" would be a more fitting term for such transmissions.

As to the question regarding information from the channel's higher self, there are many times when information received originates from that source. Most of the time this information relates to the channel's own well-being or guidance that the soulself wants to be put in the channel's conscious mind. The vibrational patterns are very different from those of the Master Teachers, however, and the channel must learn to be sensitive enough to know the difference. When knowledge is being transmitted from a Master Teacher, the higher self is respectfully silent. The higher self will often interrupt, however, if transmissions are being received from beings who are not sending viable information or representing themselves as someone they are not. Fourth-dimensional beings will often profess to be spirits of famous persons in order to get the rapt attention of a human audience. The higher self acts as what is called a "control" for the channel's open mind and guards it from interference of a negative or lower nature. Those channels who wish to receive this kind of information have the option to turn off this protection, and their higher self will grant them their wish, to their detriment, because the human entity has the God-given gift of free will.

Your Bible is called "The Word of God" because it contains inspired (or channeled) material written during ancient times by those closest to the beginning of time and those who were close to Jesus, the Christ. This is the clearest direction regarding life on your world and knowledge of the Most High that mankind has ever had during all of the centuries since its writing. It remains a wonderful work, to be revered and studied.

The Bible contains the history of the world as the people of those times could understand it, at least most of it. The portions dealing with prophecy were a mystery, eventually studied only by the priesthoods who usually misinterpreted most of it. The Old Testament was almost totally channeled through the minds of the writers by the Christ Spirit. The minds of men at that time accepted this without realizing what was happening. History that was written was written down long after it happened. The Book of Ezekiel was wholly channeled and not written by Ezekiel, but by a descendent of his who remembered stories of the happening and wished to set them down for future generations. Help from the spirit entity that had been Ezekiel was given so that the story would be accurate.

In the New Testament, the disciples of Jesus, the Christ, did do most of their own writing from their memories and experiences, but as these accounts were written years after Jesus had died, there was help from the Christ Spirit, putting into their minds the details they had forgotten.

The Process of Channeling

The Book of the Revelation was totally channeled by the Christ Spirit. John did have the dream, but as dreams go, it would have been impossible for him to recall all of the minute details that were so important for the people of your age to have now. John was fully aware that the Hand of God was upon him during the dream and while he was writing it down.

The outpourings of knowledge did not cease with the writing of the Bible, however. During the intervening centuries, many inspired writings have been given to people who were open in their beliefs and able to clear their minds of personal thoughts in order to receive inspired words to be written down for the benefit of mankind. This knowledge was given as explained above, and sometimes by illuminated thought or visions. The "channeling" done today is no different; merely a different term is used. The oracles and prophets of the Bible were channels who either spoke from thoughts, channeled vocally or wrote the inspired words.

How do you tell the difference between inspired words and misleading information?

Listen carefully. Read and listen with your mind and with your inner sensitivity and knowledge. Listen and feel within for thoughts and feelings that give you a glow of great love and peace. These come from your higher self and from the Holy Ones. Even though many highly developed souls have been commissioned to communicate universal knowledge to humanity, this does not mean that the Almighty Creator and the Christ Spirit do not do so. They most certainly do! There is no question in the mind when that happens. The extreme high that lifts the spirits and fills the heart almost to bursting are the touch of the Holy Ones, to be enjoyed and embraced to the depths of your being. Expect their touch; listen for it. We are only their messengers, at a much lower level, who are also learning, serving and climbing our pathways to become one with the Universal Source of all Things.

We send you our blessings and ask for yours.

CHAPTER TWO

Meeting Yourselves

By Master Teacher Hilarian
1993

The higher self. The conscious self. The subconscious self. These are terms that are used to delineate those parts of your true being in order to understand what, how and when you are thinking and how the system of life itself works.

The Bible terms the true being that we all are as a soul. However, a soul can be expressed in many different ways at the same time. An "expression" of the soul, or an "essence," or a part of the soul, can detach itself from the true nucleus of the created soul and incarnate itself into a human body in order to learn about life in matter. This learning process is determined ahead of time and the purpose and its options are closely watched over by the soul itself and other spiritual beings who have agreed to do so.

The human connection to the basic soul is termed "the higher self" or "oversoul." Communication with this "parent" is veiled at birth so that experiences that are planned will not be interrupted. The baby thus coming into the world starts all over again, although its general life pattern is already set into motion. The purpose of the lifetime may be as simple a thing (outwardly) as learning patience and handling emotions successfully. It may be a life purpose of great importance to humanity. Each spiritual being thus incarnated has its own important purpose for life in the third dimension, which is where the Earth is at this time.

When a human being evolves to a point where the conscious mind, the mind you use and are aware of all the time, becomes open to the fact that there is a higher intelligence involved with his or her life, a small opening is started that will eventually widen into a door that can open to the higher self. Meditation is generally the means of doing this. It takes great concentration and determination; it takes an understanding that every human being is in truth a spiritual being encased in a human body. The higher self, or soul, has the spiritual knowledge obtained after thousands of years of training and learning from higher-dimensional beings. You may have heard of sudden fantastic experiences where a person suddenly goes into a state of trance, wherein he or she is shown the wonders of time and space and knows all that there is to know. A fantastic experience! Then, a few moments after returning to regular consciousness, all the details are gone, faded quickly away. What is left in the memory is the feeling of the experience, the memory of wonder and exultation, the realization that such knowledge is really there. This is a momentary complete connection with the parent soulself. All that knowledge is what you yourself are now and always will be. The knowledge you are obtaining now will be added to it.

The subconscious mind is also a part of the soul mind that you possess. It is created and directed to provide the life force that operates your body, stores all information that you hear, see or experience. It stores all thoughts and desires. It is actually the cosmic forerunner of today's computers. The stored "hard drive" constantly sends messages to all organs, muscles and nerves of the body and directs their actions every moment of your lifetime. Science has finally "discovered" small nodules on the outside of cells that are now termed "receivers." Scientists recognize that cells are receiving directions, but what from they cannot imagine. Imagine that!

Your subconscious mind also tries to set into motion whatever program you set up for it. If you constantly react with anger to certain situations, the inner computer will see to it that such a reaction is always displayed in the emotions. That was your direction. If you enjoy smoking, your inner computer will register the pleasure you get from inhaling and moving the smoke into your lungs and set up the need for that smoke so you may continue to get that reaction, emotional or sensual. That is why hypnotism is such a recognized tool for helping someone to stop smoking. The mind must be stilled so that a strong new direction can be sent to the subconscious mind that the need for tobacco is to be negated, that the inner computer must react negatively whenever a cigarette is presented to the person. What is programed into this inner computer can also be reprogramed if there is the necessary determination.

Memory is stored in the subconscious. Science says memory is stored in the brain cells. So it is. The human brain is the computer storage unit, but without the life force that animates it, it is an empty handful of slimy ropes. The body is the organism; the soul produces the life force. The life force itself comes from and is part of creation itself – the Eternal, Superior Intelligence that is Creation and Love, that you call God. Memory is not just stored in this manner and then lost when the body ceases to live. Memory is a record of everything in the universe and never ceases. Nothing in space and time ever ceases to move and nothing is ever lost. When psychics come up with something from your past, they are tapping into what is called the "Akashic Records," which are the records of every thought, every movement, every action, every word of all created beings from the beginnings of time. This is explained further in another chapter.

So, there is a lot more to you than meets the eye in the mirror, isn't there? Each of you has an eternal, very intelligent being backing you up all the time. Your higher self is always there, trying to direct you towards your true purpose in life and away from dangers or attitudes that might cause you to fail. Pay attention to that little feeling in your chest whenever you do something you know to be wrong. That is your higher self knocking. When you listen, it will guide you from making bad mistakes and lead you to what you really want to do. If you do fail, do not feel the world will throw you away; there is always another day and, if necessary, perhaps another lifetime to use for this purpose. Otherwise, the lessons will be learned on the spiritual plane. You are so loved by your Father, the Ultimate Creator (sometimes called "the First Cause"), that nothing you can do will change that love one iota. Always another chance is given and help is waiting to be called in. The important thing is to realize that loving help is always there, if you ask for it. Oh yes, Jesus told you that. "Ask, and you shall receive." That was not an off-the-cuff statement. It is the crucial attitude you must have to receive help. Some people feel they should not always be whining for help at every turn of their road, and perhaps they are right. You are here to learn. But there is always the need to ask for strength, comfort, peace, clarity of mind, all the things you need in life to be the person you want to be. Ask for guidance in odd situations. Ask for help and protection against the dark forces that operate in the world. There is nothing, absolutely nothing, that can oppose the power of love, which is God. When you open yourself to it, surround yourself with it, nothing can truly harm you.

That does not mean that nothing bad will ever happen to you. Quite the contrary. You are here to learn to handle certain situations and if you do not encounter them, this whole thing is a waste of time. You gain in this lifetime by meeting the challenges that greet you and overcoming them. Learning is the thing.

You are a factory of machinery and energy that is running at full speed to manufacture the successful outcome of your purpose. Along the way, the purpose of learning to love and help others also has to be met. If you cannot do it one way, ask for help to see how to do it another. You will receive this inspiration in a sudden thought or idea, in dreams, by someone else "happening by" to give you the information you need. As you have heard, "God works in mysterious ways." Indeed.

CHAPTER THREE

Reincarnation Explained

By Master Teacher Hilarian
1993

Reincarnation, in this century especially, has been a concept most misunderstood by the Western world.   The first thing that comes to mind is a dirty white sacred cow being paid homage by unwashed hoards of poor Indian people.   Their concept of reincarnation is mostly mistaken also, although the spiritual leaders of that country are fully aware of its real meaning.

If you have had no prior study or understanding of reincarnation, please clear your mind and let us start from scratch.

The term "soul" is used by mankind to describe an intelligent essence or being created from the Mind of God. This being or soul starts out its eternal dance of life as a student in infinity where its education lasts for untold thousands of your years. When it has advanced to a level where a different kind of learning is required, it applies for a lifetime as a material being. This means that it will take on a period of time in a lower dimension of reality that has been solidified into matter. It will be allowed to occupy a material body on a planet somewhere in the vast reaches of the created universes, to explore the meaning of such an incarnation and learn from it. Usually, this means that the first incarnation will be into very primitive forms of life. If that upsets you, remember that this learning process is an eternal one until the created soul or entity progresses to the point of re-entry into the very essence of life, or God, that it sprang from.

A consciousness or "knowing" is in every created form of matter, be it a single-celled amoeba, a grain of sand embedded in a rock, vegetation of any kind, or the very cells that make up animal and human bodies. This is necessary so that each energy cell in existence can obey the Creator's instructions to join together in the desired forms.

The soul who wishes to experience a solid form of existence will probably enter a small animal form to begin with, to experience life on a very simple level. When that body dies, the soul returns to spirit, ready to take on a higher life form. Higher levels of existence in materiality are experienced as each prior experience is fully understood.

When your planet was created, it was formed expressly for the merging of souls into material life forms that would eventually become evolved into highly developed spiritual beings encased in higher-dimensional materiality. That means that the vibrations of mankind will increase over the ages to a point of almost spiritual form.

When animals appeared on your Planet Earth, they were of simple mentalities, obeying the natural impulses they were born with. Many souls were anxious to experience life on this new planet and gladly entered these simple forms to feel the different substance of life. Some souls were advanced enough to feel very restricted in such a life form and exited rather quickly. Others simply waited until more sentient life forms were created.

The first humanoid life forms were greeted with great delight by the myriad population of souls in the universe and they vied with each other for the honor of being chosen. Higher-dimensional beings who were their teachers in the Spirit Kingdom judged who was to be sent into this material lifetime, choosing souls with many different thoughts and feelings. There were still souls encased in the animal kingdom at that time who were able to interact with the new humans who appeared in their midst. The "new" humans explored the planet, taking great delight in the sensations of matter, feeling cold and heat, thirst and the satisfying of hunger, strength of body and the bliss of sleep for the first time. When that first excitement wore off, the sensations of sex became the highlight of their existence. They explored this in every way and to the fullest excitement they could imagine. Then they looked to the animal kingdom and began experimenting with the different species. Of course, creatures were born from these joinings that were not what the Creator had intended for His children and, from that point on, the Creator commanded that no human egg could be fertilized by any other species of life; no human sperm could fertilize any animal species. All species were limited to reproducing their own species of life, and so it is today. Humanity is having a great time trying to change this command, but will have little success.

The species of humanoids on your planet have been many and varied, and the remains of those who have not crumbled into powder are being found by your archeologists, to their utter confusion. Your present species is the ultimate form of mankind on your planet, which will not be replaced with another.

Now, it must be understood that each created soul has so much to learn to be able to reunite with the Creator, the ultimate reality, that many, many lifetimes in matter must be lived, as well as untold centuries of learning in the spiritual world. Your life is not limited to just one time around and then to the utter destruction of your mind and consciousness when the body dies. The life substance that animates the body you inhabit was not just created at the moment of your physical conception. It is already an old soul who has been immersed in the learning process for longer than you can possibly imagine. You have taken on this lifetime for the purpose of learning something that it was determined you needed to learn before you selected the parents who would bring that lifetime into the right focus. Your soul consciousness began to stay near the pregnant mother more and more as the fetus grew in her womb and, when you felt the time was right and you were ready to accept this lifetime, you entered the body of the unborn infant and all conscious memories of your soul being went to sleep. In order for the direction of your selected lifetime to proceed as planned, your soul memory remained with you as a guide and guardian of this lifetime. It is mostly referred to as your "higher self." Another aspect of your soul resides below your conscious mind and that is usually called your "subconscious mind." This part of your soul mind takes on the computer-like direction of your bodily functions and retains all memories and all instructions from the conscious mind as to the learning processes it experiences. When you learn to ride a bicycle, the subconscious mind retains the memory of how to balance the bicycle, how to pedal, brake, and so forth. The subconscious mind retains the memory of how to type on a typewriter so that after the learning process is completed, it automatically sends signals to the mind as to where the keys are so that the mind does not have to think about every key stroke.

This lifetime is experienced largely in a manner that the soul wished, if indeed the mind is open to guidance from the higher self. In some

13

cases, the ego gets between the mind and the higher self and convinces the mind that it knows better and to refuse to listen to the higher self. A lifetime of purpose can be lost this way, as far as the intent of the soul is concerned, and another lifetime may have to be entered into to try again. The functioning of the ego is explained in another chapter.

This is the last decade in which souls who are still in primary learning patterns will be allowed to incarnate into human bodies. In the new century and era of mankind that is about to burst into view, only souls who have obtained a high degree of knowledge will be allowed to incarnate into human bodies. Evolution into higher dimensions has already started. Those incarnated souls who are not able to recognize their inner soul existence will finish out their lives on Earth and then either have to wait many more centuries until other "schoolhouse" planets are available to them or seek knowledge in spiritual form.

You are seeing much violence all over your world in this age. There is a sense of desperation and futility present in the conscious minds of many that causes this violence. These people are not able to put aside their own greed or need for power to seek their inner spiritual direction. They feel time is of the essence if they are to succeed in their quests. There are millions of souls who are experiencing terrible suffering and pain in this lifetime who have come into human expression in order to complete many different lessons all at once so they will not have to face eons of waiting before they are able to make the advancement they are seeking. Does this explain a lot of things to you?

Any person who is led to pick up this book and seek the knowledge within has already felt the call of the higher self to push aside the veil of silence he or she was born with. It is time to learn, listen and experience the spiritual being you really are. This may be the first step for some of you and a continuation of the search for others. Many, many of the messengers of the Almighty Creator have been given the responsibility of teaching humanity in every way we can so that you may go forward in your personal search for the path of life. There are many who will wander in that vast expanse of eternity without direction until they finally find the knowledge they seek. You will not be one of these searching souls if you open your mind and heart to the reality of who you are and the truth you are seeking.

Every soul, at the time of entering into materiality, is also united with many spiritual beings who are joined with the soul throughout its material experience to help with the guidance the higher self is sending. These beings, whom you refer to by many names — angels, guides, teachers and so on — are able to experience the changes that are being created all the time and are able to send you on-the-spot guidance and help when you need it, if — and that is the important point — *if* you ask for and accept that guidance and help. When you have provided that acceptance on a continual basis, you will see constant little "miracles" around you all the time. Helpful small occurrences that smooth your path in life. Be aware of them and thank your helpers. You are never alone, although on a physical level, you may often feel that way. At those times, remember that you are part of an immense pool of life and that all life is related to each other by the bonds of creation. No soul is better than another; all are one in the sight of the Creator. We are you and you are we. Remember that always. We are not to be worshiped, because we are creations of soul, just as you. We have simply been around much longer and have advanced much further than you. Someday you will be in our places. Remember, even the Christ Spirit told the followers of Jesus that He was not to be worshiped. He is the highest of those created, but still acknowledges that only the Almighty Creator is to be worshiped and all prayers are to be directed to that Highest of Realities.

We are one with you in the love that is God.

Amen.

The Golden Path

CHAPTER FOUR

Remembering Your Life Purpose

By Master Teacher Peter
1990

W hile you were resting and learning between Earthly incarnations, your focus (if you were really working on your spiritual path) was on the many trials and errors made during your previous lifetimes. When a soul wishes to review its many lifetimes, it will generally focus on a specific aspect and be able to see what has or has not been accomplished regarding that aspect over a long period of time. These will flash in front of its "eyes" to give an overall impression of the aspect. If there are no faults that need to be corrected, the "seeing" goes on to another aspect, and so on. Flaws in the immediate past lifetime may not always be considered important enough to work on during the forthcoming incarnation. Instead, this overall evaluation is more important. The immediate past lifetime may have balanced out a faulty aspect in the overall picture, or that lifetime may have added a new negative aspect to be worked with in the future.

This is what has been referred to as "your life flashing before your eyes," either at death or in a near-death experience. During an Earthly incarnation, only the immediate lifetime is reviewed in that manner.

The process of review may take only a few hours (your time), or it may take centuries, according to the need and the spiritual purpose of the soul. Sometimes the soul will wish to observe conditions on the Earth plane to see where it may want to fit in a new lifetime, what could be accomplished, and what benefit its presence might have to humanity at the chosen period. Many souls wait for centuries in order that their own particular abilities and talents may be used at the right time.

Souls whose bodies are violently destroyed by war or evil purpose of others come into this dimension very angry. They have been denied the time to work out their purpose for that incarnation and are sometimes very resentful. Instead of taking the time to realize what the reason might have been for their destruction and what their destroyers' motives were, some souls shrug away all offers of help or guidance from their teachers and angels and force themselves back into the world without due care of where and when.

These poor souls often find themselves in circumstances where, as a baby, they are unwanted or cared for very poorly. There is no direction for the child, since it has not set the direction before its birth. The many homeless, wandering young people of today show their resentment by violence upon others without realizing they are trying to show their anger at their own violent deaths, thus creating a circle of cruelty and injustice. They have allowed their feelings to crowd out the natural love and creativity that still resides within. Only occasionally is an enlightened soul able to reach their inner selves and draw them back to reality in time to correct the lifetime. The recent wars on Earth have thrown many, many souls into this position, not just in your country, but all over the world. A woman raped and killed in Asia may rebirth in America, thus causing additional confusion in the new lifetime. An American soldier may return as a child in China and be resentful of the extreme lack of personal freedom. Although these souls send themselves into their new lives, their teachers, more and more at this time, will send them to areas where they will face challenges undreamed of, which will inevitably teach hard and valuable lessons, reaching past the anger and confusion.

Your present era is one of very hard lessons. There is little time in which to face the necessary challenges and work with them. The hard facts of life are harder; the deficiencies are more intense; the stress and heartbreaks hit deeper and last longer. Your Father is not being cruel to you; you are souls that have taken on this lifetime in which to learn more and become more than you are. This lifetime was known to be coming and those of you who are privileged to be living in it are those who have planned, some of you for ages, to be reincarnated now. The spiritual path is a long and hard one. Many souls wander on and off of it many times, delaying their eventual oneness with the Eternal One. Those of you who are trying hard to deal with the difficulties of your life will harvest unimaginable success and progress upward on your path and perhaps will return to help those struggling with the events to come in the new era just about to open.

Do not think that because you are aware of this spiritual reality you are something special. Look carefully at the people you know and work with, your friends, your not-so-friendlies, your employers, governmental representatives, etc. Each incarnated soul is aware deep within of what it is here for, even if the conscious mind blindly goes its own way. That deep awareness contains the lifetime's instructions, its memories of other lifetimes and experiences, and that part of the Living Awareness, love and Creativity called God that is part of every soul. No matter how hard an entity tries to shut out the inner urgings, they are still there, trying to find expression in the soul's life.

Mankind has tried, for centuries, to close out those thoughts and urgings, forging hard walls of indifference, hate and cruelty. If the entity passes from this lifetime without breaking down those walls and coming face to face with itself, there will be long periods of reviewing and teaching before the soul will be able to search out the right lifetime to learn these lessons over again.

The Hitlers of the world come back into spirit in a black cloud that takes a long time to disperse. They inhabit a dark place where their lives are mirrored to them until they can no longer stand the image and cry to the Most High for help. Then the help is given and the teaching begins again.

Where does one begin to search within? Anywhere. All around. *Everything you are reflects in everything surrounding you.* Are there angry quarrels raging around you? Look at your own attitudes. Are you causing the situations that create the quarrels? Is it hard for you to make friends? Perhaps you hold your inner beauty and love inside so that others cannot feel it and respond. Can you be giving and open to yourself as well as to others? If you have responded to old training that taught one should not be proud or generous to oneself, then there is a wall that will prevent you from seeing yourself as you truly are.

To truly go within, first one must see clearly the feelings, abilities, attitudes, needs, desires and goals that every human embodies within the conscious mind. Realize that these feelings have not just been created during this lifetime, but that they have deep inner backgrounds that have evolved over the centuries, in some cases. For the most part, humanity believes that a baby is born, learns to walk and talk, goes to school and learns the necessities of civilization, then works with what has been learned for the rest of its life. How sad that mankind has limited itself to that extent! Every soul entity has many abilities and talents learned over many lifetimes just waiting to be released and used again.

In the past 50 of your years or more, older people who now have the time and money to do as they like, are experimenting with new crafts or arts and finding talents they had no idea they had. The new sciences and computer systems are pushing young people as never before to use the hidden abilities at much a younger age than anyone ever thought was possible. Humanity has limited itself to the mundane. When soul entities open themselves to the possibilities of almost unlimited ability, then will humanity attain the progress it aspires to.

When the soul entity has recognized its mental self to the point of acknowledging the inner self, the process of going within can be started.

The only pathway to the soul is silence. The mind must be trained to release all thoughts, cares, fears, planning and expectations. Even beautiful positive thoughts need to be stilled. When this has been accomplished, you might focus on a candle flame, a light, a flower or some beautiful single object, in order to keep your quiet concentration intact. This will gradually lead to a complete stillness. In the stillness you will find a love and peace beyond anything Earth can conceive of.

Within the stillness there will be comfort, serenity, guidance and whatever contact with the upper dimensions you have come far enough to attain. This will not come easily or without much determination and effort. To walk the spiritual path takes a firm commitment, not to be broken. It is part of every soul's lesson to be learned in each lifetime. If it is learned, then the soul's purpose in that lifetime will be revealed, the soul entity will be able to see what it has done or not done, and guidance will be easily recognized.

For the time being, information that is being released to the world through many channels is giving sufficient guidance for mankind to adjust itself to the demands of this age. However, in the coming years, this information will become more highly structured and intense.

The purposes for which incarnated soul entities have devoted themselves will become almost explosive within if the entities have not opened themselves to them. This will create almost unbearable pressures in many people who will not understand what is happening. These pressures will cause many to look for help and find friends who will explain the problem. Others will bend to the pressures and become ill or react with violence.

To some extent, this is already happening in some parts of the world where unreasoning violence is causing upheavals and misery for millions of people. Mind-conditioning of populaces by many negative governments and military organizations is only a part of the problem. Inner pressures are accelerating and those in countries which do not acknowledge spiritual patterns have no outlet for these pressures; these people are not helped to look to themselves for the answers, but only to obey governmental commands so that "all will be well." Unfortunately, that answer only exacerbates the problem.

Pressures and tensions that exist today in highly educated business and personal worlds are only adding to the inner pressures that are building up. It is no wonder that mental illness and breakdowns are very common and it is sad that such mental torture must be experienced before the soul entity relents and seeks out spiritual help. Even those who have never had spiritual training eventually raise their hands in surrender and plead for a God to help them. God is there; the help is there.

Infants being born now are, obviously, very old and highly developed souls who are being sent especially to help those who do not use their inner resources to help themselves. They will be teachers for the most part, and also highly skilled scientists who will lead the world to the realization that what seems to be obtuse because it cannot be seen, felt or measured is in reality creative energy making up the universe. This unseen energy will become the driving force for all material needs on your planet. The new era will have no need of created electricity or power created by gas or coal.

These newly embodied souls will know their purpose for their new lifetimes very well; it will be a part of their personalities. Their learning processes will be guided entirely toward their inner goals. A child who has destined itself to be a spiritual teacher will project its learning towards good communication skills, involvement with people in all walks of life and skills in understanding all cultures and religions. Music will be important to a teacher, for in music speak the angels to the inner self.

One who destines itself to merge the knowledge of matter and the knowledge of the higher dimensions will turn its attention at an early age to mathematics, drafting, engineering and the like, as well as to understanding the spiritual backgrounds of those it will work with. Those who will work in governmental capacities have even the greater responsibilities of teaching those in authority to understand the true laws of living together on a large planet in peace and unity. They will have to learn communication on a background of love, understanding and practical knowledge of all governments in the past. Only those who have, in past lives, ruled communities or nations themselves will have the ability to successfully take these positions. The Christ Spirit will be taking control of the world in those times and these new souls will be working under His direct guidance, with full knowledge that they are doing so.

Yes, there will be many now living who will also be working under the Christ Spirit, although very few will really understand that they are doing so, just that they are being spiritually guided. They will be especially blessed, for they are those who are following their inner guidance without having direct knowledge or contact. This is the faith the Bible speaks of with great feeling and love.

Let us speak of the illnesses and disasters that fall upon so many people, now and in the past. It is extremely hard to bear a child that will always be disabled or disfigured, or to see someone you love crippled or rendered helpless by an accident or willful injury to them from someone else. Always is heard, "Why did God let this happen!" The Almighty and loving Creator did not let it happen or cause it to happen. In most cases the incident is just that, an accident. The soul entity must then expand its efforts not only to achieve its soul purpose, but to contend with the extra lessons it must learn in order to cope with the situation. I have said before that sometimes the teachers of soul entities will set up circumstances for their pupils in order to broaden their experiences; this is also a possibility in such extreme traumas. In many cases, the soul entity itself has entered a lifetime that will produce a body that is not normal in order to experience the pain, anger and frustration that will occur in that body. This is a hard lesson to learn; those who succeed with such an experience will learn patience, love and the overcoming of bodily sensations. They will use the time and experience to overcome worldly confrontations and enter into themselves to gain contact with their higher selves. Many people who are unable to communicate with their fellow beings are highly skilled at communicating with their spiritual teachers and their Creator. Although they may seem pitiful beings to most, know that they are soul entities who are becoming very aware of what is around them and dealing with difficult situations in ways a normal person will never know. Almost every soul entity has had an experience like this in some lifetime. If not, the entity has gained knowledge that equates to a lifetime as a handicapped person.

Be very kind and loving to severely handicapped people. You will receive a great reward by the response in their eyes. They are very aware of love and caring thoughts. Ugly thoughts and pity are terribly unsettling and uncomfortable to them, as they are in a mental world of love.

Remembering Your Life Purpose

Those who have been thrown into a life of pain and injury will seem to have lost touch with reality for a time. The transition is devastating. Here again, sometimes this is just an accident that the soul entity will have to face as a greater challenge to cope with. Sometimes the life pattern has been set by the soul entity in order to understand what others have gone though or will go through in the future. How can a teacher understand the pain of others if he has not experienced it fully himself? Many future teachers are undergoing lifetimes of pain or incapacity in order to understand the feelings of future pupils who will be undergoing similar lessons of their own. The new era will not be too much different as to the lessons that need to be learned by those entering that lifetime, but spiritual help will be available whenever it is needed or asked for by the new teachers who are being born now.

Trace your own beginnings in your meditations. Yes, this can be done. When you have attained the point of contact with your higher self, you will be able to inquire about certain lifetimes, preferably in the context of learning the background of a certain ability or, perhaps, a hang-up that you are unhappy with. You can receive this information. Those who have evolved far enough will be able to review the reasons for choosing the present lifetime, to rethink their present life and see where they can do better to follow their purpose. More and more soul entities are attaining this level, raising the vibrations of your age to a level that is most pleasing to the Creator. It is surprising to find that you were once a primitive Indian, moving quietly through a thick forest to avoid wild animals; a serf in the Middle Ages cutting wood or tending a cook-fire in a castle; a slave working in the fields of the Old South; an Asian woman washing clothes in a muddy, mosquito-ridden river; a Chinese coolie carrying rice in baskets suspended by shoulder poles. Do not expect to see yourselves as great rulers or famous persons, although sometimes you will. If so, try to pick up on the great lessons learned during those lifetimes. Did you fail to bring peace and prosperity to your people? Did you learn well how to understand and rule over the lives of many? Did you learn how to deal with the burdens and tensions that a real ruler always has to contend with? What did you learn from those experiences that will help you now?

What did you learn from the poor people? Patience, how to deal with frustration and resentment? How to fend for yourself and make do with what is around you? Skills now perhaps lost?

Every experience in the body leaves new skills and lessons; every experience entails mistakes and actions that are not well remembered; these are lessons too.

You do not have to actually remember all these things to benefit from them. For example, if you see someone hurting another, and you have been hurt yourself in a distant past, there is the immediate need to help that person and stop the attack. You cannot just look the other way and ignore the situation. If, however, you have endured terrible injustices or injuries and the hurt and resentment are still in your subconscious memory to an explosive point, you might side with the attacker and egg him or her on.

Your underlying memories have a great impact on the current lifetime. There is no action you will take that does not have a relationship to everything you have thought and done in this lifetime, as well as in all prior lifetimes. Your higher self is the vehicle that sorts all of this out and guides you around the situations you meet in life. Only on a very high level is a soul entity able to cope with these prior experiences and not feel overwhelmed by them.

In the time it takes to read this lesson, your conscious mind, your subconscious mind and your hgher self have been comparing notes, so to speak, to guide your way of thinking, your reaction to these words, your ability to weigh wisely what you have seen and to help you bring it all together in the best way possible.

Discovery of yourself and your higher or inner self, floating over the boundaries of time and space, is the most fulfilling experience any soul entity who incarnates into a human body can possibly have. Once the mind has flowered into awareness, nothing in everyday life can be too much to cope with. One is aware of those loving beings who are with you at all times to protect, teach and guide when asked to do so. This eradicates loneliness and fear of the unknown. Instead of fearing what might be, the soul entity can know that all will be handled with the love and Power of the Creator, working together with it. Love is the overpowering force that fear cannot fight against.

Every soul's purpose in taking on embodiment is to learn.

The most important thing to learn is how to love, first, the Almighty Creator that you term God, then yourself, then the rest of humanity. Love cannot be passed on until it is perfected within the self.

We send you all our love and our knowledge. Use it the best way you can to help you on your path to the Light.

Given with love.

The Preferred Path

By Master Teacher Hilarian
1991

A long the paths that are the probabilities of each step taken during a lifetime is a pathway we may call the "Preferred Path." This is the way of action or thought that is set before an individual that translates his or her life purpose into the right action. When there is the opportunity of choice, inner guidance will always point to this Preferred Path.

This has to do with conscience in a way, but the inner voice of each spiritual being has with it all of the guardian angels, teachers and spiritual guides that are working with the embodied spirit to strengthen that "nudge" toward the pathway that will lead to completion of the life purpose. This is very important to know, to realize that life's choices are not all that scattered and haphazard. Life in the third dimension is given for very definite purposes. A soul entity is not just dumped into any old place and time, then left to fend for itself. After the decision is made to reincarnate in order to learn specific lessons or for specific reasons, spiritual advisors are set into place to be with that embodied entity to help it achieve that purpose or reason for being. Each lifetime is a very directed period of time in a soul entity's existence and the importance of following Preferred Pathways is paramount in the success of the "mission."

When a psychic looks into the future of any person, what is seen is the pathway that the individual is headed for at that moment in time. Five or ten minutes later, if that individual goes out onto the street and meets someone who talks him or her into some new project or undertaking, that pathway is immediately changed. For each minute, hour, day or year of your life, there are uncounted pathways for your life to take. Everything you hear and learn, each person you meet or speak to, all ideas and actions play a part in making decisions about what to do, how to act or what you think. It is like a kaleidoscope, constantly changing with each movement in time. Life in your dimension is in constant flux, with myriads of choices to make every day. How, indeed, to know when you have chosen wisely; how do you know when the Preferred Path is in front of you?

Unless you have awakened to the inner voice of wisdom that is always present in all of us (yes, in the spirit world, too), there is no way that you *can* know for sure that your feet are on the Preferred Path. If your mind is still sleeping, you have no way of knowing that there is a purpose in your life. How often do you hear, "What am I here for?" Almost all human beings have the inner feeling that there must be a reason for life and many search in all the wrong places for the answer. Without knowledge that the answers are within, that meditation is the doorway to such answers, it is extremely rare that an answer will be found.

In order to sort out the many ways to be traveled, one must maintain a constant state of listening within the mind and heart. Prayer and meditation are the tools you need to create this pure attitude. Harmonious and positive thoughts are what turn the feet in the right direction. Inner guidance that is perceived directs the thoughts and actions to the Preferred Path for your purpose. It is as simple as that.

If and when you fall captive to the negative thoughts and actions of others and are taken in by them, the doorway to guidance is firmly shut and the gentle hands that lead you in the right ways are not able to touch you. It is your own choice here in what you want to think and do that determines the guidance you will receive. When thoughts and ideas are pointed towards negative ventures, the Holy Ones cannot help you, for your gift of free choice from the Creator is always the ruling factor. Be very careful when making choices.

There are times when a bad choice is made without thought or simply out of ignorance. This does not cut off your spiritual guidance, because you have not done it purposely. When confusion sets in because of that choice, simply relax and ask for help. It will come and what to do about the problem will be made clear.

Even in the most trying and difficult times of life, even after giving up on yourself and the whole world, there is still that small nagging voice within urging you to ask for help, somewhere, somehow. Many dedicated souls are embodied to help and teach those in dire distress. They have discovered that this is their purpose in life and they make themselves available when the need is there. Sometimes it takes another who can remind the errant entity of the guidance that is available and show them how to listen to it and receive it. God's love is never "turned off;" it is always there for each of His children. But, it is the child's choice either to receive or reject it. In rejection lies a lifetime of frustration and unhappiness, for the inner being knows that the lifetime is being wasted; the soul entity is not doing what it embodied to do. That disappointment flows through to the conscious mind and is reflected in the depressed attitudes of the individual.

When the soul entity refuses to try to accomplish the purpose for which it embodied, there is a pressure to find something, do something, to fill that empty gap, that unknown something in the far reaches of the consciousness that constantly nudges the mind. The unreasonable urge for money and power is a good example of this. There is never enough; there is always the need to push further and further, whether or not money and power are really needed and regardless of others who may be hurt by that relentless advancement.

The inner purpose of embodied mankind is to learn to love God, to learn to love yourselves and to learn to love all others without restriction or judgment. The responsibility of each entity is to take care of the body it is given and to be caretakers of the beautiful world that was created for God's children to be their schoolhouse. No, it is not easy. You would not be here if it were easy; that is the point.

Again, use prayer and meditation to hone your awareness of inner guidance. At first, it will be very subtle, then, as you listen and obey it, the urges and voices will become much clearer. As in anything else, awareness of inner guidance has to be learned and practiced before it becomes a really viable force in your life. Take the time, even a few minutes a day, to tune in to that inner guidance.

Really listen, and you will be surprised at what may occur. Your spiritual counselors are always on tap, ready to jump in whenever you are ready to listen.

Finding that Preferred Pathway is your road to real happiness in this lifetime. You will feel a sense of accomplishment at times without being aware of what you have done! Peace within your inner being will be realized; love will surround you and everything you do as a matter of course. Following the Preferred Path will become such a right thing to do that all other paths will seem shallow, unnecessary and downright uncomfortable.

We love you all. Call on us and we will answer.
[Note: See the chapter entitled "Learning to Stay Inspired" in Ken Carey's book *Terra Christa*.]

CHAPTER SIX

Meditation for Everyone

By the Beings of Light

T here is no time like right now to consider learning how to meditate. This practice will not send you into outer space, put you in a state of complete trance or make you look like a dweeb (or any other current nerd-word).

Meditation can accomplish several things, according to your need and intention. It is a way of getting rid of modern stress and tensions. It can help you get in touch with your inner being. It can be a direct line of communication with the higher-dimensional beings who are always with you, guiding, suggesting and helping you along the path of life, and it can put you into a state of total communication with the Creator of All Things.

During the time you are in any of these states, you are still able to be completely aware of what is going on around you; you can hear, feel and see (if you have your eyes open). You have simply stepped up your mental conscious awareness to a point of being more fully aware than you were before.

Why would you want to meditate? Perhaps you need to find a way to relax your mind and body because they are threatening to go out of control or not responding as you know they should. It is necessary to rest the body when it is overtired and, similarly, it is also very necessary to rest the mind when it is overloaded. Just like any machine that is not taken care of regularly, the mind can find itself in a state of confusion or simply refuse to remember the things you need to know.

Let us take you through a simple way to relax to enter the first stage of meditation.

1. Make time. Early in the morning; in the middle of the night; when the kids are in bed; any quiet time you can find. A quiet place somewhere in nature is excellent — wherever you can be undisturbed for at least 20 to 30 minutes.

2. The Eastern religions use a sitting position with legs crossed and hands lying quietly on the knees, palms up. The feet are tucked into a rather difficult configuration if you have not been trained for years to do it. Why this particular position? If you seat yourself in this manner, you will notice that you feel balanced and relaxed, without much danger of falling over. The hand position is meant to bring the meditator to a balance of energy. The hands contain nerve and sensory endings that constantly bring new energy into the body. By relaxing them in a palms-up position, you are giving permission for new energy/information to flow into your mental and physical systems. If this does not appeal to you, try sitting in a comfortable chair that supports the body and head without strain. Many people also lie on the floor with a small pillow. Remember, however, that your subconscious mind has been trained since you were born to think that a supine position is meant for sleeping, and it is very difficult to try to meditate without falling asleep. Try different positions and see what is best for you. One thing is important, however, and that is to keep your spine straight, whatever position you choose. Energy travels through the spine and for really effective meditation, that energy should flow in a straight line. Slouching is a bad habit anyway.

3. Breathing is a natural function of the body, of course, but most people have fallen into rather bad habits about it and breathe rather shallowly. If you live in a big city, that has some good points. However, in order for the body to absorb adequate oxygen into the bloodstream, deep breathing (from the diaphragm) is the way you were meant to take air into your body. Meditation requires a good supply of oxygen to the brain, so the first thing to do is breathe — deeply. Fill the lungs, hold the breath for a few seconds, then exhale — completely. After a few

times, you will start to feel a bit light-headed, probably; then go back to "normal" breathing. When you are exhaling from the deep breathing, let your muscles relax, a little at a time.

4. Now, this is the time to quiet the mind. Tell yourself that you are giving your mind and body a little vacation for just 30 minutes. Tell your subconscious mind to quiet down and send no mental messages for that amount of time. Tell your conscious mind to be quiet for 30 minutes. Concentrate your full attention on your feet, telling them to relax, toe by toe, if necessary. Next, do the same for the legs, thighs and hips. One leg at a time. Work through the entire body, one area at a time, your choice. Work the shoulders and neck muscles, the head and all the little muscles around the ears and eyes, at the last. You should feel like a lump of lead, with nothing capable of working at all. Perhaps a rag doll would be a good analogy. Your mind is now quiet, for you have pushed everything away except the concentration on relaxation.

5. Listen. How often how you been able to listen to complete silence? No thoughts — no strain. There is immense beauty in silence. Listen to the solar wind, the stars, the unseen energies that move all about you. Flow with the silence and float in it. If you hear far-away voices or music, or see flashes of pictures, accept them and keep floating. They are nothing to fear. When the time you have set aside is coming to an end, you will begin to bring your conscious mind back to the body and take on normal feelings again. You have given this instruction to your subconscious mind and it will take care of your return to normal consciousness. Only this time, the body will feel relaxed and your mind will be more peaceful and clearer.

That's all there is to the basic principal, and if that is as far as you wish to go with it, fine. This method of mind relaxation will help you do whatever you wish to do in your life with greater clarity and determination.

Now, if you wish to achieve higher consciousness, learn to be psychic, be able to communicate with your spiritual teachers or delve into the deepest depths of your own spiritual being, meditation is the only way to accomplish these things.

Just as in anything you do in life, there must be a clear idea of what

31

you wish to accomplish. Spiritual consciousness is no different. You cannot believe you can just dive into the ocean and immediately know how to swim. There must be the conscious determination of what you want to do, how you are going to do it and when you are going to do it. The universe has very definite rules and regulations which are followed by all created universes. Creation is instituted in specific codes of order and if the steps are forced into unnatural patterns, there are either bad results or simply unordered confusion.

The first and most important thing you need to learn is about yourself. You are not a clump of living clay some unknown life force turned on, that returns back to nothing after its existence is completed. You are an immortal, spiritual being, created by the Eternal Supreme Intelligence you call God. The life force that you are is made up of the air itself, swirling about you all the time. The cells of your body are constantly being renewed and recreated. The attributes of your being were built in when you were created and are yours for all time. You can think, create and, most of all, love — for that is the reality of your being. Love. You are never alone, for other spiritual beings are always beside you, helping and guiding your lifetime in matter. That inner conscience you are generally trying to ignore is the sum total of the guidance you are receiving. Listening and following those sometimes vague feelings is the most important thing you will do in your lifetimes. The more you listen, the clearer they become. They will never guide you wrong. No matter how loud and insistent are the media and the human voices that try to tell you how to live your lives, only your own inner guidance will tell you the unvarnished truth.

Your being is made up of three parts. The higher self (or soulself — your real base of operations); the conscious self (what you are thinking with now); and the subconscious self. The subconscious self lies deep within the conscious mind and is your managing computer, so to speak. It is programmed to run the body, play back the responses you have programmed into it and keep in memory every word and action, every sight and sound you experience during your lifetime. It is a repository for every bad habit you have programmed into it. If you are trying to quit smoking, you are bucking your subconscious.

You can reprogram your subconscious through meditation. Remember, the first rule is to decide what you want to do. If smoking is something you wish to stop, that can be accomplished. In order to change subconscious programming, a very deep meditation must be entered into. At the point where everything is silent and deep, start concentrating on what you wish to change. It is best to use a few concise words, over and over again, as long as you can keep the concentration. Example: "I no longer have the desire to smoke." Depending upon the individual, this should have a very prompt response. You would see the desire for a cigarette lessen after just a few sessions. There are many ways given to do this with chemicals and so forth but doing it yourself will end the whole thing and give you an inner pride that cannot be purchased over the counter.

Many habits can be altered this way and each time you succeed, it will be a tremendous boost to your self-esteem. Your new clarity of mind will help you understand what you need to do next.

As you work within meditation, using concentration and learning to listen to your own guidance in many ways, you will begin to notice that what you wanted to accomplish in the first place is starting to happen by itself. When the mind is rested and clear, what you term psychic knowledge or events will begin to happen naturally. The word "psychic" is simply a term denoting the spiritual abilities and knowledge that you already have. Being psychic is simply letting those abilities happen. You cannot learn to be psychic, because you already are.

As times goes on, you may very well begin to hear voices in the silence, sometimes only one or two words. It may take some thinking afterwards to figure out what they meant, but that is generally the purpose of it. Little pieces of advice or knowledge will come through from your higher self or from other spiritual advisors. Sometimes the "voice" will be like a regular sound, or the voice will be a "knowing" in the mind, or a strong thought not your own. Keep listening.

"Flashes" or small visions may flit through your mind, yet remain clear and concise for a long time. These often consist of pieces of another lifetime —yours or others'—on the bands of time. They are interesting and mysterious. If your intent is to learn something of your prior lifetimes, put that intention in your mind as you drift into a deep meditation. Your higher self is always there to help you in whatever endeavor you wish. The more the concentration is held at a particular level, seeking a particular thing, the more success you will have.

Meditation is a way of life. You have probably heard of being in "constant prayer." This does not mean that a person shuffles around on his knees all the time, but is a state of recognizing that the life force is a part of the Living God, and, as such, is also in constant communication with that Living God. It is a mindset that is always aware of the small nudges and helpful guidance that are constantly a part of our beings. Meditation can become so easy and so everyday that one may slip into a two- or three-minute session at odd times and still benefit tremendously by it. It is a way of making an answer clearer or of talking to your spiritual teachers about something important. Edgar Cayce liked to say that prayer is speaking to God, and meditation is listening for the answer.

Answers, however, can come in many ways. Some people never hear a word, never see a vision, but still feel the love, caring and understanding in the silence. Look back on the past year and realize how many times you have been helped in little "miraculous" ways. Things that just couldn't have happened, did, and they started to happen all the time. Every time you acknowledge the help you receive, the more your spiritual helpers are around to give you more. They have no ego problems as you do, but appreciation and love make the universe as well as the world go 'round.

We have been telling you about meditation in a very general way, giving some common examples. But realize this: Meditation is an extremely personal thing. Each and every person will experience it in a different way. Your myriad experiences all through your many lifetimes have molded you into singular beings that have no equal in all of the created universes. Your training in the present lifetime has further added to the spiritual beings you are. What you will experience then, deep in meditation, is given according to your own spiritual totality and can never be experienced by anyone else in exactly the same way.

The purpose you have taken on for yourself in this lifetime is being helped along by your spiritual counselors and many times the words, thoughts or visions you receive will have something to do with helping you achieve that purpose. If you have gone far off your path and are in some kind of danger, warnings are sometimes given in a way that you can understand. Whatever you receive from the higher dimensions are tailored for your benefit.

It must be remembered that although the experiences during meditation are extremely clear and sometimes remarkable, upon awakening they will rapidly start to fade away. This is because you have been in a higher-dimensional space and these things do not relate too well to the conscious mind. It is like the dream state — very similar. Until you have disciplined your mind to remember, it would be wise to keep a journal of some kind nearby and record what you have experienced immediately after the meditation ends. A day later, you will be glad you did, for otherwise it would have been gone.

How does all this fit in with your normal world? Not too long ago, people who meditated were treated as kooks and thought to be pretty weird. Things have changed and are changing rapidly. Huge seminars around the world are teaching people how to relax by this means and many large companies have meditation rooms set up for their employees, which is an excellent idea. Fifteen minutes of meditating rest and clear the mind far better than a smoking break! There are few people today who deride the idea of learning to rest the mind and body. Some religions still believe this has something to do with the devil, but then, they have probably never tried it.

There is a warning to be given. When an individual opens his or her mind to the higher dimensions, there are always those beings in spirit form who are looking for that opening. Sometimes a spirit being refuses to return to its spiritual home and is insistent upon living on Earth. It will sometimes try to enjoy that life through a still-living human being. Occasionally this results in what is referred to as "possession," but today we see that happening far less often than in the distant past. The intelligence level of humanity has come a long way in the past 100 years and most people know instantly that something is wrong if some other force tries to take them over. Usually, this "takeover" will be on a simple level of trying to enjoy smoking or drinking, for those terrible desires and drives do not simply cease upon death of the body, but linger on in the living personality. It may take many, many Earth years before the entity can release these desires and be able to fully relax into the Kingdom of Love that surrounds it in its spiritual home. Let that be a another brief warning.

If you receive, during meditation or at any time you have opened yourself to a higher consciousness, information that seems scary, unreasonable or false in any way, or seems to direct you in negative ways, break off contact immediately. Direct prayer to the Creator and ask for protection and/or put the white Light around you. This will send the wayward spirit away. Better to wait a few days before trying again, while keeping yourself surrounded by love. Remember, there is nothing in Heaven or Earth that can withstand the Power of God! Fear is in the mind of man, not the Mind of God.

There are many meditation tapes on the market today, and they can be of great help. It is difficult to concentrate on the mechanics of working with the mind when the day's problems are whirling in an unending spiral in your mind. The tapes help to give the mind something else to listen to and directions to follow. The relaxation sessions are a good way to learn how to release the tensions of the day and the visualizations are fun and sometimes very inspiring. There is a matter of "too much of a good thing" here, however. You can spend the next ten years working with these tapes, but never get closer to your inner self. When the silence is achieved, the mind and body relaxed, turn off the tape and proceed as directed above. These tapes make a lot of money for their authors and most of them are made with the best of intentions. But, they cannot do for you what you can do for yourselves! We see far too many groups using interesting tapes during group sessions when they should be combining their meditative energies on a specific thought or project.

Meditation, properly used, results in a strong force of energy. It has to, to achieve what it does. When two or more persons combine their time and energies at the same instant, that force becomes even more powerful. Peace initiatives, awareness of the need for the preservation of the Earth, the stopping of possible atomic wars, all have happened because of the combined strength of millions of people meditating and praying together. There is nothing so beautiful as the peaceful and powerful feelings generated by a meditating group of aware people. This is what truly pulls people together in love and trust. There can be no spite or hate or deception in such a group; it is a healing and growing force of love. This is why small groups accomplish so much more. One does not attend such a group unless he or she has the intention of growing in knowledge and awareness. Large church groups contain many people who attend for social or political reasons and the cohesive energies that cement the small groups simply do not exist. If you cannot find a group where you live, try to find one other person who is willing to study, pray and meditate with you. In a short time, others will find you!

We'd like you to consider this: There are times in the lives of you all when everything goes wrong; when seemingly unreasonable and unaccountable accidents happen that completely turn your lives and the lives of those you love around and shake the very foundations of life as you know it. You are told over and over that everything that happens is because you created it, one way or another. For the most part, this is true. But there are accidents. There are terrible things happening in your world that have nothing to do with you or your own determination of where your life is going. The variations in the endless multitudes of tiny events occurring every moment of time are too complicated even for those of us in the higher dimensions of time. A lifetime that has been well planned out before incarnation can be completely upset and destroyed because of a simple mistake or accident caused by someone else. Yes, this happens. That lifetime then becomes an even greater challenge to the entity whose higher self gives as much help as possible to make a learning experience out of it. This is not all that tragic, however, since each soul entity lives through countless lifetimes in many dimensions, many times and many planets. It is normal that a few of these lifetimes fail in one way or another. If this has happened to you or someone you love, it is time to realize that new plans need to be made for that lifetime; it is time to release old desires, needs or plans, and time to look ahead for the viable possibilities that lie ahead. If a lifetime in a wheelchair, for instance, is substituted for a sports career, it takes some extremely strong intentions to quiet the rage and grief and the difficult determination of learning acceptance. Then, and only then, will the inner being be able to start sending new guidance and help.

Meditation is the best way in the world to regain the balance such tragedies destroy in the human spirit. It is not an escape from the cruel, cruel world, but an entrance to new strength and wisdom. Living a very physical, busy and productive lifetime is wonderful, but the benefits of living a very mental lifetime have given the world new technologies, beautiful music and wisdom beyond compare. Life is much more than a beautiful face and a strong set of muscles. When you have visited your higher being in meditation, this is easy to realize. One of the most accomplished mathematicians in the world cannot move his body at all, but his mind has given the world what a physically able man could not.

Meditation can be used as a point of concentration for the mind and subconscious mind to heal the body. It is no secret today that the mind controls the body. Emotions, hatred and resentments are making a mess out of humanity, but humanity is beginning to realize it. There are many fine people, doctors and clinics who are working with people to help them use their own minds to heal their ills. Meditation is the key factor here, for the intense concentration used in these methods is the only way to absolutely reach the deepest parts of the mind that control the bodily functions. Using this method yourselves, before you become ill, is simply constantly affirming that your body is in perfect condition, functioning as it should and that there is nothing that can harm it. Don't you think that would work?

Just try it over a few months. You will never feel so well.

Look at meditation from many angles, and you will see how much the human race is beginning to learn and depend upon it for the truth and knowledge that is sought for so earnestly now. Every man and woman needs it in different ways and will benefit from it in different ways. Search your heart, your desires and even your physical needs to see if this is not something that will help you.

There is never a time when your need for an inner commitment to yourself is not important in your life. Living your life as though you were forever sailing in a boat on the ocean of life and never knowing or understanding the myriad life forms beneath you is foolish and boring. Too many people have lived and will live their lives this way, searching, always searching, for something exciting and worthwhile, while all the time it is really there, inside them, and they never know it. We sincerely hope you will take on the adventure of the totality of life, within your-selves, in others and in the recognition of the ongoing creation of life itself.

God bless you all.

CHAPTER SEVEN

The Ego

By Master Teacher Peter
1990

Among the diversities of living in matter is the almost impossible enigma of what is called the ego. It is the most important part of a human personality, and yet the most difficult to deal with. To begin with, the ego can be thought of as a layered set of recording discs, as in the computer we are working on. They record all thoughts and feelings and are in constant motion. What they give back, however, is something entirely different. The ego does not just record thoughts and feelings, it magnifies them, sometimes changing them according to its own whims and making a disconnected mass of intentions and desires. Why? Why did the Creator give the human family such an erratic facet of its personality to deal with? That, of course, is the answer. The management of the ego is a very large part of learning to live in a sensible, comfortable manner.

An undisciplined person is one who merely drifts along and lets the ego rule in any way it desires. The result is a person who drifts through life without direction, without care or thought for others, and completely open to thoughts poured into him from the dark forces. The ego has no conscience; it does not hear the inner guidance and direction of the Christ Spirit; it has no loving care for the entity it dwells within. It is like a mixed-up computer, without direction from an operator. The soul entity's first responsibility is to gain complete control of the ego, to make it work for the benefit of the entity.

How? By being very aware of your feelings and your reaction to them. Give yourselves a little space away from what you are doing and feeling and look at this very carefully. Are you able to control your anger, jealousy, hurt feelings, thoughts of being what you are not? Ego is used a great deal to express the inner blowing up of a person's importance far beyond what he or she really is or can do. Ego can also pull a person down into the pits of despair. This all happens when ego is not controlled.

Awareness of your feelings and the determination to take them in hand is the first step. You are not alone in this battle of the mind; your angels are your first line of defense. Ask for their help to erase the hurt feelings from slights that may have been tossed at you. Ask for help when anger bursts forth, unasked for and frightening; it will be calmed. Ask for help when others complain that you have become overbearing or "snooty" in your relationships with them; you will be able to sit back and look at yourself. It is important to see yourself as others see you. This takes a bit of self-discipline, but is a very important necessity in your lives. It is the same as looking at a problem or an argument from only one side. There is never only one side; the universe is too variable and too much in motion for that and this also applies to every thought or action in human life.

For example, let us look at a young girl to whom her parents give little encouragement or praise while she is growing up. Her ego reacts and sends hurt feelings, depression, a sense of inferiority to others. She is caught between the parents and her ego and feels there is no place to go. Her guardian angel comes to her rescue and tells her to look around and observe others, that she has talents and abilities that are just as good and important as other people's, even better in some cases. The angel talks to her ego also, and commands it to let up a bit and give the girl some inner feelings of importance; the realization that her parents have problems of their own and cannot fulfill her needs sometimes. If the girl accepts these thoughts and begins to work with them, she will begin to control the negative thoughts from the ego and come to terms with them. Thus the ego will start to learn how to search through the mess of negative input and begin to put it into identifiable categories, to be dealt with by the girl. Ego can be disciplined, taught and used as it was meant to be. Beyond the ego is the inner mind and the knowledge you are all born with. When you reach for the truth, it will be found, for it is there. When extreme difficulties seem to overwhelm you, reach for the strength inside your being to deal with it; it is there. Ego is merely the clearing house for all thoughts and feelings that constantly come and go. It is up to the soul entity to learn how to organize it and make it work in its favor, instead of letting the ego gain a confused control.

Deny the negative thoughts the ego magnifies from the world around you. You are aware of negative thoughts and ideas every time you pick up a newspaper or turn on the TV. You do not need to take them into yourself. Train your ego to recognize that these things exist but that you will have nothing to do with them. Instead of hiding under the bed every time someone taunts you or puts you down, remember who and what you are and command that your ego protect you from the hurt feelings. No one can erode your feelings about yourself but you.

There is no need to pretend to be what you are not. It is a matter of recognizing realistically your good and your bad points and living your life in an aura of confidence and love. It is not hard to do. When there is a difficulty with the personality, ask for your angels to surround you with clarity of thought and you will be able to see clearly where changes need to be made. Do not discount or ignore the fact that you have guardian angels. They exist and are assigned to help you all through your life; they are your best friends.

It is very lonely on top of a mountain. One who lets the ego set him or her apart as being too important or too knowledgeable for others will find himself or herself without friends to talk to or be with. This is not a natural state of affairs for a human being. He or she needs the love and companionship of others all the time and will emotionally starve to death without it. Look at the lonely people you know. Their spark of life is very low; they have no interest in anything and draw into themselves while their ego continues to pound them into nothingness.

Love is the root of every good and beautiful thing in the universe and is the very energy you are made of. When love is directed into the ego, it immediately gets busy organizing feelings into correct order. It has no other choice. Love is the builder, the organizer, the deep presence of God, which no ego can fight against. The Presence will direct the negative thoughts and feelings out the door and your inner being will be happy and well again, without the heavy sense of pressure in the chest. Dread of the unknown, of bad things to happen, of being left behind will disappear. You will gain the certain knowledge that you are an important being in the universe and can handle anything that comes your way. Reversals are to be expected in life, but they will not pull you down; you will merely take another turn in the path and go another way. This is part of the learning process you are dealing with. With the help of those spiritual beings that are always with you, you will emerge from the battle of being with your head high and your heart singing the praises of the Eternal. Control of the ego is the secret of winning the battle of life.

Call on us; we love you.

The Golden Path

42

CHAPTER EIGHT

The Akashic Records Explained

By Master Teacher Peter
1990

There is a small space in the universe called the Fields of Time. This place is reserved as a universal record vault, created to store all vibrations of every event, every thought, every word spoken, every law made, every movement in time. You call that storage center the Akashic Records.

Your scientists are realizing that the atmosphere itself stores such movements and thoughts in vibrations that surround certain areas. When high-energy events stir up the vibrations to a certain point, they tend to remain stagnant in an area for many centuries. However, they are also duplicated in the Fields of Time as a matter of universal law.

This field, though I have called it a small place, would be equal to three of your universes. It is a small place in relation to the eternal scope of all that is created and all that is not. Only the Eternal One can even conceive of the vast reaches of time that are still empty space.

Within the field, there are many angels whose job it is to arrange in categorical order the material constantly coming in. They have been there since the beginning of time and are very efficient at their job. The responsibility of maintaining this huge information bank was delegated to one who is called the Master of the Records. Directly under his supervision are two recording angels who oversee the fields in two sectors.

They are directly responsible for the eternal retention of the vibrations. The working angels maintain contact with all areas of the universe and each one is assigned to a different area. Does this sound like a huge corporation of some sort? Remember that patterns of arrangement and conduct did not originate on your planet. They have been in place forever in the Mind of God. Mankind has finally understood them enough to use them in Earthly affairs.

Why is such an information bank necessary? Why all that work? Just as understanding your own planet's history is so important to understanding it today, all that occurs in the universe is vitally important to all those who inhabit the world of spirit. Time as you know it is nonexistent in the fields and future happenings are recorded as well as past and present. As you may assume, all events are in a constant flow of change, as circumstances dictate from moment to moment. The angels see to it that when a record is consulted it is up-to-date at the moment it is called up for viewing. Every civilization on every planet has permission to consult the records in the fields as soon as they have advanced enough to do so. The Akashic Records are open for all to see when the soul has advanced its vibrations high enough to be able to see.

Please realize that what you call "memory" is a part of the Akashic Records. Although your records become a part of your subconscious mind, they would not have the ability to remain in your mind if they were not reflected by the fields. All memories of a soul are in the field. Your philosophers correctly intuited that the fields exist and called it "universal mind." A very good term that was. Your subconscious mind is also able to use that information when it chooses, without your conscious knowledge.

When a hypnotist regresses a subject back to another lifetime, the purpose is generally to correct an unpleasant condition in the present. The subconscious will search the prior lifetimes of that particular soul entity and release the memory of the time that created the problem into the conscious mind of the subject who is in an alpha or higher mental state and able to receive it. However, when a regression is done for the purpose of finding an interesting or important lifetime, the subconscious, always very obliging, will search out such a lifetime from the Akashic Records that will please the soul entity. That lifetime will not necessarily be one that the soul entity actually experienced in the flesh.

Many people experience flashes of scenes from the Records in meditation or even during waking periods as visions. This happens when a person's vibrations suddenly surge to a point where he or she touches the fields or is helped to do so by guardian angels for one reason or another. The memories encountered may or may not be his or her own. Is this done to confuse the soul entity? Let us say that it is a part of the training experience to be able to recognize the seeing of the Records for what it is, instead of feeling they have suddenly become superpeople.

Visions of the future are obtained from the Akashic Records by those who seek them, who simply pull these visions to themselves by a sort of magnetic energy, and by those who receive them suddenly, without warning. These sightings are not given without reason. They are controlled by the soul entity's higher self and its teachers in spirit. Akashic visions are also learning experiences that the human mind must learn to work with, deal with or learn to ignore, depending upon the situation. Knowledge of the future is also given to certain people for prophetic purposes, as it has been down through the ages. If it is heeded, humanity is given a chance to change the future if it can.

It is almost overwhelming to realize what the Records accomplish in their entirety. When a petal falls from a fading flower, it is recorded so that the seed from the flower will be directed to fall to the ground to grow another flower. When an animal dies, it is recorded so that its essence may be retained and returned again to the Earth. When an Earthquake occurs, it is recorded so that the balance of the planet may be retained in proper order.

The fields are in place to keep order in all of created matter and all that is not yet created. The fields are a repository of the existence of all created soul entities, where they are located, their progress along the Path of Light, their purposes and their assignments from the Creator. Nothing is ever lost in time; all is known by the Creator through the fields.

Knowledge creates balance; the balance of the universe is maintained by the fields. Your Akashic Records are far more than you have ever realized. They are there for you to use. All knowledge is there for you to obtain. The fields exist in your section of the universe and you are surrounded by them. The knowledge that your world desires is all around you in what is called the "ethers." It takes only a sincere desire, an open mind and a high rate of vibration to pick it up. The Creator has made the whole procedure very simple for His children, when they are ready for it.

This is the reason that your teachers, guardian angels and guides are able to find answers for you very quickly when needed. All the answers are there, open for viewing for all those in the higher dimensions. They need only to seek to find. Ask what you will, when you are able, and all knowledge is yours for the asking. This is part of what Jesus, the Christ, was saying when He said, "Seek, and you will find." Do not hesitate to ask for information. If, however, your advisor knows that your having such knowledge will cause you trouble or will cause trouble in general, it will be withheld; the advisor will tell you that it is not available at the time. There are also things regarding the future that mankind is not allowed to seek out for its own good. Rely upon your advisor to give you what is acceptable for your benefit at the time requested.

The "ideas" and "revelations" that people receive are, for the most part, derived from the Records. However, there are many soul entities in spirit who wish to pass along their own knowledge and experiences and relate them to the human mind in this manner, especially those of a creative nature. There are very highly developed beings who wish to gift the Earth with beautiful music or literature to improve the receptive centers of the mind, and who also endow the mind with their gifts. Beethoven, the deaf composer-musician, was one of those so gifted. Some writers have entire works of literature running through their minds like the screen on this computer. Almost all creative endeavors are derived from events or mind-pictures from the Records or friend-entities in the higher realms. That is not to say that creative endeavors are not also the result of the soul entity; they are. They are merely helped along when the creative vibrations start working.

This is but a small explanation of the workings of the Fields, but perhaps enough to give awareness of their vastness and the necessity for them. The Creator's Kingdom is a most intricate creation and most of it will never be understood by His children. We can but accept what has been so generously given and be eternally thankful for it.

Given with love.

CHAPTER NINE

The Law of Karma

By Master Teacher Kathumi
1993

The word karma comes from Sanskrit, the ancient Hindu language; the English language really has no word that describes this concept. The concept of karma, simply put, is universal law, always in place from the beginnings of eternal time. It says that whatever you do creates a forward force. This force sometimes pushes up against another force that makes it turn around and fall back on you. If not, then it keeps going until it ends up in a circular manner and comes back on you from behind. The prayer wheels in Asia demonstrate this truth. There is an understanding that "what goes around comes around."

Jesus, the Christ, put it this way: "As you sow, so shall you reap!"

Every thought, every action and every intent stays in motion. The nasty name someone calls another does not just fade away after the sound has ceased; the word, the intent, the emotion behind it combine to be installed in your memory, the memory of the recipient of the word and in the everlasting records of time. It becomes a part of your own Book of Life, there to stay until it is erased.

Sometimes this negative action or thought comes back in the form of bad luck or someone else striking back from the insult, bringing you trouble and grief. Sometimes it simply stays in the records until your return to Spirit. Then, it becomes what is called a "karmic debt." This means that until you have corrected the matter by doing something that is just the opposite in another lifetime, the stain remains on your soul.

Why do soul essences continually return, life after life, to learn on Planet Earth? Most of the time, it is to do penance for the mistakes in another lifetime that must be erased. A man who has hated people of color and maligned them all his life returns the next time as a Black child so he will understand the hurts and traumas that he gave to someone else. This new lifetime is not forced upon him; this is what is seen to be necessary in the spiritual realm. Murderers, thieves and so forth often come back as those who will be the victims of other murderers or thieves in order to suffer what they inflicted upon others.

There is a balance in all things. The Creator of all worlds set into motion certain rules that are never changed until the Holy One decides to change the whole pattern. All patterns are based on balance, and life on your planet is no exception. Good and evil are always balanced, for the evil one does does indeed live beyond into the dimension whence that soul comes. Negative action or intent must be reversed in order to achieve the balance that the soul has to have before it can continue on its long journey of understanding and knowledge to become at last one again with the Superior Intelligence you term God.

There are terrible wars and suffering going on in your world now that will continue for another decade at least. Millions of people are caught in situations where they are absolutely helpless to help themselves or to change the circumstances and madness that swirls about them. Why are they there?

For thousands of years spiritual entities have incarnated into human bodies in order to face the negative forces that dwell upon your planet. The negative forces (called the Devil, Satan, the Dark Ones, etc.) are necessary to give the challenges, enticements and urges that mankind is there to deal with. When these things are overcome, the soul has proceeded another step toward its goal. Now God in His Plan will, during the next few decades, stop the inflow of soul entities into your world who are not highly evolved beings. Those who really want to use your world to be able to erase many stains upon their life records are coming en masse to be reborn in disastrous situations so that many stains may be erased at once; they may not have another chance. Learning can be done on the spiritual level, of course, but the solidity of the lesson in matter is powerful indeed, and this hard-won harvesting of wisdom means many fewer centuries are required to erase the stains.

There are some cases where mistakes are made and individuals suffer these tortures without having to do so at the soul level. Is that so shocking? Not really. They are learning the terrible things humanity has faced and will face for some time to come, that they may return on a higher level to teach and heal. A teacher or doctor is much better able to help someone when the hurt of the other is understood.

A child is born to a couple who decided to have a child because they hoped it would save their marriage. The entity who wishes to help the two people understand more fully what they are doing will be born into that baby, but stay only long enough for them to become very attached to their offspring; then it withdraws and leaves the couple with a dead baby. When something like this happens, it has nothing to do with the karma of the baby, but with that of the couple involved. There were hard lessons to be learned about love and responsibility.

I would not even try to give examples of the millions of other situations involved in the karmic law; they are infinite and of infinite proportions. Every time one person interrelates with another, there are karmic laws at work. One or both persons are interacting constantly with situations that affect them both. Each situation that is encountered in life has something to do with events that point or will point to certain steps that will or will not be taken. Sound confusing? To the finite mind it always will be and it is senseless to try to track any one instance down too far, for it will become so intertwined with so many others, only a computer as large as the universe itself could untangle it.

It is enough to know this: for every action, there is a reaction. This is not new to you, but it goes much further than the old textbook phrase. Whatever you do will come back to you, one way or the other. A frown will affect others the way a stone tossed into a pond creates rings flowing outward. Eventually, however, those rings will reach you and the effect will make you feel as downcast as that original frown did someone else.

Smile, and the world smiles with you. (Lots of these gems!) Strange, that no matter how many people disregard and deride universal laws, the language for them is rampant in your society. A smile and a loving look is the most contagious disease in the world. Seldom is a smile not returned, for it gives the receiver an inner lift. If someone is so down in the dumps he cannot respond, send him a quiet prayer for strength and peace. He will feel it.

The good that you do also comes back to you in unsuspected and surprising ways sometimes. Those who spend their lives giving of themselves to others are seldom oppressed with negative feelings or doubts. Picture life as lived in a handball court: a bad serve can come back and knock you out, but a good one will bounce just where you want it to and make you happy.

As you continue to study, you will find many books on the subject of karma that will further explain any questions you may still have. Universal laws are written in time and cannot be broken, whether you like it or not. They are beautiful laws when they are heeded and obeyed.

God bless you.

CHAPTER TEN

Out-of-Body Experiences

By Master Teacher Hilarian
1991

Have you taken a trip into the cosmos lately? A lot of people have — even just a little trip around the block without your body falls into this category. You call it an Out-of-Body Experience, or OBE.

Many people experience this spontaneously, without thinking about it or training themselves to be able to do it. This indicates that the ability has always been very strong in their personalities during prior lives and has seeped over into the present lifetime without their being aware of it. It can be a very natural occurrence or cause a great deal of fear and worry.

It is very disturbing to have an experience like this without understanding what is happening or why. The trauma of such a mental trip has driven many people to psychiatrists and doctors, trying to find answers. Some are lucky enough to find them from such sources.

An OBE, once experienced and understood, can be a very heady experience that one wants to delve into again and again, deeper and deeper. Floating around the neighborhood, seeing what the neighbors are doing and then telling them about it later is a real lark, but that grows dull after a while. The realization grows that if one can separate from the body, might it not be possible to float up into space? Of course it is, and the silver cord that connects one to the body is always there for the traveler to return by. Returning is easy in this phase; you only need the thought to go back to the body, and there you are. This is a very conscious OBE and one that is entertaining and pretty safe, as far as the conscious mind is concerned. If you are able to take trips like this, fine. Enjoy them. It can do no harm if you do it in moderation. Of course, if you are so wrapped up in it that you spend most of the time with your body laid out in bed while the rest of you is speeding around the galaxy, the whole idea of your embodiment on Earth is being defeated.

There is another way to have an OBE, and that is when the consciousness slips into a higher level of awareness and enters the fourth dimension. The geared-up consciousness then leaves the body and enters realms of dimensional awareness that can be extremely frightening. There are realms between dimensions which such travelers sometimes wander into that contain souls and conditions that have not as yet earned the right to exist in the fully dimensional realms of the Father's Kingdom. You call them "demons" and "devils." The atmosphere is extremely negative and a traveler can be attacked by these beings. The silver cord is still there, but the act of returning can be hampered by the inhabitants of these realms, and getting back can be a very frightening experience. Mr. [Robert] Monroe found that out when he entered these spaces, and it took him a long time to understand how to deal with it.

No, a spiritual OBE is not always like that. What is encountered relates very much to the soul entity's position on its pathway to the Light. If this is a very educated being, highly enlightened, who is coming near the end of the myriad lifetimes it has experienced, the spiritual journey will probably be one into the realms of Light to visit temporarily with friends or relatives or do some thought-out traveling. This being would be aware that such trips are available, but that the real trip and experience must be on Earth.

So, is it wise to train yourself to take out-of-body trips? Here, I must say that it all depends upon what you expect to receive from such mental excursions. If you are doing it for the "grand experience" (translated — for the fun of it), you will be spending a great deal of time training your mind for something that will not be beneficial for your Earthly purpose. After all, the time allowed for a soul being to be embodied is a very precious time. The entity chooses the time and place for the incarnation in order to work out spiritual lessons that have to be learned. If this much time is wasted in trying to get out of the body, what is going to be learned from the Earthly experience?

Of course, studying and learning all one can about the spiritual kingdom is part of the process of enlightenment that an embodied soul should learn. Learning at the third-dimensional level seeps into the soul being much more rapidly and becomes a very deep knowledge that can never be lost. That is why Earthly incarnation is so very important. Learning in the spiritual realms tends to be more dream-like and is sometimes lost in that higher consciousness. Knowledge of how to enter and return from the body in matter is often learned as a matter of course when the enlightenment process is activated, but at that level it is understood how, why and when to use the ability.

Drifting up into the higher realms can be a revelation of wonder and a matter of understanding that life is eternal, not just a short time to be lived in one body. With the advent of current medical accomplishments, many, many people are now being brought back from the spiritual world after being dead for a short time. When the body is in dire circumstances, the functions of the body slow down and in some cases stop. Although the body is not yet entirely dead, the soul personality starts leaving the body. This is to prevent the pain or shock from penetrating the consciousness of the person; it is a gift of the Creator to spare His children the sometimes terrible pain of separation. When the body is saved, the personality, most of the time, will return to finish the purpose for which it came. There are times when the personality refuses to return and the body will die despite the best efforts of the medical team. During that brief time of separation, the wide-awake consciousness of the personality is fully aware of what is going on and sometimes travels quite far into the regions of time before it is evident that the body will survive.

It has certainly taken humanity a long time to accept the experiences of such revived personalities as real and not hallucinations. The consciousness of the soul entity never sleeps and is always aware, on a higher level, of what is going on, whether or not the Earthly consciousness is awake.

Before deciding to go into a training situation to be able to go out of your body, please think it over carefully to determine what your real purpose for this is. After all, you really already exist in a higher dimension and you are here for a very important reason.

What happens to your higher self when you lift out of your body? If you have not come to the point of connecting consciously with your higher self, it simply is there with you, trying to guide and help. If you refuse to listen to it, perhaps as usual, you can get into difficulties just as much in the higher realms as in the world of matter. When you are out of the body, this guidance is very much with you and you are able to feel and listen to it more openly than when you are in the body. At this time, you can find a beautiful connection of love and caring that will carry over when you return to the body. This is one good reason for an OBE. It is not necessary, however, since when a person is truly studying and meditating, that connection can be reached just as easily in other ways. Will the higher self turn you back and restrict your movements while out of the body? No. You are still operating with free will and that cannot be overridden by any soul, even your own. You are still in charge and must make your own decisions.

If you "lift out" without trying to do so, do not panic. Use a few minutes to experience the freedom of spirit and to realize that this is who you really are, a spiritual being, not the body you see beneath you. Give yourself time for this truth to really penetrate your being and rejoice in it. Then, just direct your thoughts to returning to the body and you will be there. Sometimes this gift is given to an individual by the higher self in order to give this realization. It need not be repeated if you do not wish it.

Some persons, hearing and reading about the experience, really want to be able to do it, but have no success. Very often, there is no necessity for the experience when they are fully aware that it is possible. These people know their spiritual heritage and it is not necessary for them to explore realms they know they will be returning to. It is a knowing that is also called faith.

Make your own decisions and know that help is always there when it is asked for. Even in regions of the scary unknown, God is there. Love overcomes any dangerous situation, and you can return with that loving help.

In the meantime, make the most of your time in the third dimension. It may be many thousands of years before you may return to it again.

We all send our love and blessings to you.

CHAPTER ELEVEN

Déjà Vu •
Synchronicity •
Angels •
Anticipation

By Master Teacher Hilarian
1992

F rom the past often come many memories of past lives, or sometimes events shock one to the foundations of the mind as the
event is duplicated in current time. "There is nothing new under
the sun" is an old saying that has great validity. From the trillions of
combinations of events occurring through time, in each lifetime almost
everyone experiences this at least once. Of course, it is called "déjà vu."

Coincidence is another matter. Happenings coming out of the blue
that relate mysteriously with things one is thinking or doing do not come
by themselves. They are generally set up by your angelic friends who feel
you need a slight shock to make you remember or to emphasize something. This is also called "synchronicity" by people who are aware of
spiritual influences on such events. As the angel legions come into the
world in larger numbers now, expect to experience more of these mind-
joggers. They are meant to help, guide and remind you that there are
angelic beings around you all the time, making the way a little easier or
interesting.

Search out in your minds the times when an angelic presence has affected your lives in one way or another during your lifetimes in this galaxy. Being "lucky" is a recognition of that presence; having a sudden inspiration is an angelic presence feeding you an idea that will be beneficial to you. Something heavy not hitting your toes as it falls sometimes reveals an angelic hand at work. When their small gifts are recognized and they are thanked for them, your angels feel uplifted and will try to find even more ways to please you. They are messengers of God and try to follow through on answers to prayers you have sent that the Creator has instructed them to act upon. You need to think of them as beautiful, loyal friends who are always around when you need them. If you are really fortunate, you might be able to see them, in one form or another. Many appearances of angels are with the beautiful wings that you generally think of as being attached to their shoulders. That is a fantasy, of course, but it is a beautiful sight and they are happy to oblige. Usually, the appearance is of a large, shining figure in a white robe. When you consciously call them, there is usually an immediate warm glow of love surrounding you. What a nice way to begin the day.

The ego dearly loves to put its ideas of grandeur into such appearances or occurrences, and the next thing it will do will be to think about telling everyone how terribly psychic you are or how advanced you have become now that you are receiving spirit visitations and making wonderful things happen. Watch out here! To really connect spiritually with angels or any other spiritual being in God's Kingdom, one has to "shift into neutral," so to speak. The conscious mind cannot anticipate what might be given, as it is not wise enough to determine what is best for the emotions. Anticipation of God's mercy and love should always be in the heart and mind, but keep the possibilities open. Too many mental pictures of what you want will block out what you really need to be given. Similarly, any negative thought whatsoever will nullify what might have been. In the spiritual world, negativity is a powerful force that creates a rightful balance in the universe. When it is used by the conscious mind, however, it becomes extremely dense and acts as a wall to the ambitions and desires of mankind. Anticipation is a beautiful open way of worshiping your Creator. It is an opening of the hands to receive the gifts that the Father is so willing to give and has promised through the Christ Spirit. Receive what is given with a grateful heart and understand that even when the gift is one that creates hard times or heartbreaks, it is given for good reason. Learn to accept what is given and train yourselves to stand back and see a difficult situation with the attitude of something being created by it. Looking back in retrospect, you will see many events that were terrible at the time but ended up creating a new outlook on life, perhaps, or catapulting you into new ways of living or new careers. Life is not easy on Earth and mankind has to learn to cope with it in many ways. Your spiritual counselors are with you every step of the way so that the end product of each lesson will advance your knowledge or thinking. That is, if you let this happen. Fighting against people and events only postpones the lesson. Meet life head on and be ready for any gift, be it wonderfully surprising or a traumatic blow.

Do not confuse anticipation with expectation! The two words are similar, but their meanings very different. Building up expectation in your minds of what is to happen is a very dangerous mode of thinking. How many wasted days, weeks and months have you not wasted looking for what you have predetermined will happen? Expectation is a human way of trying to trick fate into obeying your desires and what you determine as being the best thing for your path through life. Human expectations are very faulty because a soul entity encased in a human is quite unable to see the future view of the consequences of actions and events. Your spiritual teachers and angels can see ahead and know quite well what action will produce what reaction. Anticipation is a way of opening your heart and mind to whatever is the best for you, as determined by those who love and guide you. Acceptance goes with anticipation, accepting whatever is given, even though it is not what you may have expected. Know that whatever is given is for your continuing education on Mother Earth.

No matter what you experience in life, the love of the Creator constantly circulates around you in the very air you breathe. Breathe deeply many times during the day, and that special energy will invade your body in wonderful ways. Should the air be polluted with gases and unpleasant organic matter, set a mental image of a filter in front of your face that takes out the damaging material. This has to be quite intense, to be sure, but it does work. The pores of your skin breathe also and that love energy flows through you as it flows through every living thing. Kathumi has much to say on this.

When the energies of the planet are especially active and at high peaks, there will often be felt a tingling on the skin or on the top of your head. Nothing is wrong; that is just stronger energy entering your body and your crown chakra. There will probably be an inner rush or gradual increase of your own energy, or perhaps the mind will seem clearer and you will want to get busy and do something. From now on, this may be expected; you will get used to it.

Your mind is a wonderful instrument, an electronic computer created at the beginning of time. Remember, the same principle applies. Garbage in, garbage out. Be selective as to what you let enter that storage bank of memories. There is a lot of garbage in your world today and you need to learn to set up a filtration unit in your mind to keep it in good shape.

The world is changing very rapidly and so are the minds of human beings. Intelligent thinking is on the rise and those who feed their minds the right information will be those who will fashion the world to come.

We send you our special blessings.

CHAPTER TWELVE

The Path to Enlightenment

By Master Teacher Peter
1990

Where does the feeling of extreme spiritual bliss come from? How can one feel detached from the body and soar to heights never before imagined? What is the force that lifts your spirits and separates one from all Earthly cares and troubles?

It is your own inner spiritual self.

Every soul incarnated on your third plane of existence carries with it its own memories of the spiritual existence in the higher planes and, even clothed in flesh, it yearns to return to the love and peace of that beautiful home. The need, almost constantly, of a feeling of security and love dwells deep in the human mind, unknowingly echoing the forgotten memory of what truly lies within.

This lesson will try to assist you to awaken that memory to some extent to enable you to feel that security, love and peace that dwells within. When you wake up in the morning, if you don't have to hop out of bed immediately, try to stay in the "twilight zone" for even a few minutes. If you are still within a dream, try to think about it for awhile to see what it means to you; if not, just lie there and keep your mind open, without drifting to the day's schedule. This is a time when your higher self can reach through to speak to you or send images that are meaningful to your life. It is a time when you can touch that part of your soul that is hidden during much of your conscious daily experience.

As you continue with your morning activities, try to keep in touch with your inner self and your higher self by being aware of your feelings toward anything that happens. If stress and anger appear, try to take a few moments out to feel what is really happening; take clues from your inner "voice" to help deal with the situation. There may be a very strong push from within to admit you are wrong, even if your stubborn ego absolutely does not want to say such a thing! Perhaps ego wants to stay aloof from sharing some deep feeling or thought with someone else, but your inner voice is telling you to let loose and give the other person a part of you by sharing the feeling or thought. The term "uptight" actually means more than just a tense situation; it also means that human beings are often trained from childhood to keep their emotions and real feelings to themselves for fear of being ridiculed or pushed away. This happens, of course, but remember, this is the other person's way of defending or covering up his or her own emotions and feelings for fear someone might peer into his heart and find that he has beautiful thoughts, too! It just isn't the "in" thing in many strata of society to be spiritual or caring; an overlay of false sophistication, an air of knowing everything important to know and nothing else being important must surround the person. Do not let this kind of arrogance stop you from saying what you feel and what you mean. The time for putting on false faces is past. Strike deeply with the truth, no matter how brutal the response may be. Know this: the truth penetrates deeply into and behind the arrogance and pretense; there is no defense from the truth. It cuts and eats into the listener's mind and heart, never to be forgotten. For, in fact, the same memory of the true spiritual being lies in the inner consciousness of all incarnated souls. That truth will connect with those memories and cause them to start rising to the surface. That will cause the actors to have feelings that will surprise them and give them uneasiness. Hopefully, they will be pushed to the point of finding out more. This is really the first step of becoming enlightened: listening and being aware of the inner soul being that you are.

The second step is to study the words of teachers from the beginning of your recorded time. There are many works written before the Bible, but they may be hard to find. If you cannot locate any of them, the Bible is the best starting point. Compare what you read with the Bible; it contains truth. Truth, however, has been limited in some cases and removed from the Bible by those who wished to gain control over masses of people. Read the Bible with the knowledge that you are a spiritual being, created of the Almighty and Everlasting Spirit that you call God, that you take on human flesh many times, that higher-dimensional beings have always communicated with those in the flesh to help them understand the laws of God and fulfill their purpose in living this life, and they still do. From that viewpoint, the Bible comes alive again and the knowledge in it vibrant and important.

Knowledge that has been sent from God's messengers to humanity is overflowing in books now. Information is transmitted in many ways and from many different viewpoints. Why? Knowledge is given so that each of you may find it in the way that you can understand and relate to. If the material is offensive in any way, discard it. If the material seems too far above your head, lay it aside; some day it will be clear. There is so much to learn in this closing of an age; make time to study and learn.

Have you found others who are trying to learn also? Good. Gathering in groups and discussing what you are learning is the best way. Become close with each other so you can share feelings, misgivings and the spiritual thoughts and flashes of insight you may receive. Sharing with others clarifies what you think might be just imagination. Learn to trust in what you feel and receive; it is very subtle and easy to overlook. You must acknowledge that it was heard and did exist. Hang on to the subtle receptions; think about them and see how they relate to your life and feelings. Most communications received in this way are to help you in your relationships, your problems or your way of thinking. Even a few words heard unexpectedly can turn your life around. Listen. Listen.

After you have studied and made the determination to become much closer with your inner being, it is time to start meditation. In your studies and in prior chapters in this book you have come across many different ideas and ways to commence meditation. Try them and see what comes most naturally to you. Over the centuries, you have done this many times and there is probably a certain attitude and position that will feel most familiar and comfortable.

It is difficult in your world of stress to find a quiet time for meditation. Making a living, for both men and women, requires dashing to work and back, preparing meals, caring for children, keeping up the home, participating in social and community activities and so forth. Where is the time? It is very important to make time. Some people program themselves to wake up during the night and meditate for 20 minutes or so; then they fall asleep again. Their sleep is even deeper after meditating. Some get up earlier and go into another room for a brief meditation before the rest of the family awakens. During the day, if there is such a place, perhaps a few minutes can be found in a park or quiet rest area. When one really has the need and the determination, a time and place will be found. Those who have retired from the workplace to a quieter way of living are fortunate; they can choose their own time.

Group meditation is a wonderful way to get in touch with yourself and your higher self. The energies produced when several people meditate together help boost the energy levels of all. It is a most beautiful experience. Do so when you can.

Now, what do you do with what you are learning? Hug it to yourself and walk around with a superior air? Hopefully not.

To have higher spiritual knowledge than others means that you must teach it to others. You don't have to get on a soapbox in the park and sound off or open a storefront church. What you do in your life, how you react and relate to others is how you teach. How you give yourself in situations where you are needed is how you teach.

Do you have to give up going to church when it does not teach what you are learning to be truth? No. If you feel comfortable in that church, stay with it and learn what you can. Your teaching, again, will be in what you say and do. Many so-called church people say one thing and do another. By your conduct, you can be an example of saying and doing the same thing.

Are the rites of the church, such as baptism and the Lord's Supper, still valid and necessary? Yes and no. The rites that were instituted by John the Baptist and the Lord Jesus, the Christ, were meant to focus people's minds on what they were learning, a way to verify to themselves and others that they accepted the teachings of the Laws of Truth. Having babies baptized, as was later instituted by the churches, was the act of parents promising to teach the Word of God to their children as they grew up. It had no effect on the children, of course, because they were not able to make such a commitment. After children are grown old enough to study the Word of God and understand it, at least to a simple degree, then they are old enough to give that commitment, be it by baptism or other rites. Baptism should be the performance of a person giving himself or herself wholly to the commitment of the Laws of God and giving the heart to God in love. It should be a personal commitment.

The Lord's Supper, or Communion, was not instituted by Jesus, the Christ, as a rite to be performed every Sunday or every month. It was to be done at a meal, as He did it, a time of quiet gathering or solitary thought, in remembrance of Him, as He said. It is not wrong for a church group to do this, of course, but it should not be thought of as the only place to do it. It, again, is a personal act, an act of remembrance and love.

The Path to Enlightenment

Wine is required, if you truly wish to recreate the eating and drinking in remembrance of the Christ. A small sip is sufficient. It is a beautiful thing to do and when the mind is stilled and you are truly thinking of Jesus, the Christ, you will receive an inner glow of love not to be missed.

Every religion has its own special rites and sacraments, and when one is studying to find deep inner truths, it is well to think clearly about what you are doing when performing these rites. If they feel comfortable to you, continue. If you feel uncomfortable, do not continue with them. If these rites were created to worship the Father, none of them are wrong.

Each person will reach enlightenment in his or her own way. Some will reach a point where personal communication on a conscious or higher conscious level is possible; others may not. This is not that important to each individual. Reach as high as you can; feel the communion with the inner part of you that is a part of your Creator and the Christ Spirit. It is beautiful and loving; you need never feel alone. Be a part of all creation around you, love it and appreciate it. (That includes all incarnated souls, you know.) It is impossible to love a lot of people, at least on the outside. Love them for what they truly are, even if they don't know it. Send love when they communicate hate, envy or pure nastiness; it will make them feel ashamed. Send love when they are down and withdrawn; they will feel it and it will make them reach for more love. Send love when you feel ridicule; it will dissolve the worst in people. You will not look foolish, they will.

Enlightenment means simply that you will feel lighter in your mind, your soul and in everything that surrounds you in this life and your inner being. It is a knowing that you are an eternal being who has just recognized itself for what it is and this is the most wonderful "high" of all! Let that Light shine out from within you and others will feel it and be drawn to you in ways you could never imagine before. That is why the term "Light Workers" was born. It is impossible not to feel that Light of God coming from them. It is difficult sometimes not to close it in when adversity and anger are around you, but that is the time to send it out.

We are always with you to help, advise and protect. Just ask and the Christ Spirit, and His servants and messengers will always answer to give you inner strength and love.

Given in truth and love.

The Golden Path

CHAPTER THIRTEEN

Changes

By Master Teacher Peter
1990

T he Glory of God shines forth in every created thing. When you
sing of the Glory of God, you are recognizing that the Creator of
All is a Shining Being whose Light transcends any other light in
all the reaches of eternal space. We are now using the word "Light,"
capitalized, to express that glory Light.

Light, as we are using the word, is much more than just a shining
brightness; it signifies the Knowledge of God, the love of God, the shining
forth of the ever-increasing vibrations of those who are learning, following
and living the Word of God, as expressed by Jesus, the Christ (in many
different roles as universal teacher), the Bible, the spiritual knowledge
stored by many peoples over the centuries and by the spiritual knowledge
being transmitted to humanity today. This is "walking in the Light."

How do you know if you are indeed walking in the Light? There is an
inner glow that permeates your being when you are truly on the beam.
There is a sureness in your thinking and decisions. There is the inner
knowledge that the Father of All is watching over you and that what you
need in life will be provided when and in the way it is needed. It becomes
easier to send your love to someone you dislike, knowing that the bad
expressions of personality overlay the old soul underneath. Meditation
becomes easier and the time spent in meditation is a time of utter
tranquility and love, making it hard to leave it for the everyday chores that
must be done. You are repulsed by the negative patterns of life around

you and do not wish to see negative programming on television or read about it in the media. The thought of war and the agony it entails brings tears, even to your inner being, and your prayers increase for the enlightenment of those who even contemplate it. Your preference for reading material shifts toward books that contain spiritual messages.

Yes, you will change dramatically. Your thinking in the present personality will undergo a transformation that your family and friends cannot fail to see. Your every step in your new life will have a different meaning and your way of expressing yourself in every facet of your life will change. You will see the ordinary things in a different way, be able to see behind the outward manifestation and pick up vibrations of thoughts and emotions much more clearly than ever before.

Awareness of your body and its needs will become more important as you realize that it is your responsibility to take care of it properly. It is your "vehicle" that takes you through your life. If your vehicle wears down and cannot function, your purpose for this lifetime will falter and fail.

How will this affect your relationships to those around you? Your family will see their loved one change into a person they like, but it will probably bother them that the "old" you has disappeared. If they do not or cannot share your new wisdom and knowledge, there will perhaps be resentment and a pulling away. This is not easy for the one who walks in the Light; it is heartbreaking and many marriages fail because of it. Remember, a personality will draw to itself another like personality, and when the differences become too great, there is a failure of communication. The love may still be there, but the resentment and misunderstandings overshadow it to a point where it is imperative to seek out those who are also walking in the Light.

A soul entity who is raising its vibrations must either try to help those around it to do the same or realize that some of his or her friends and loved ones will be left behind. That is simply the nature of things. Classes of people throughout the ages have separated themselves not just because of their financial status, but because of their mental vibrations and knowledge. An understanding flow of energy must pass between those who enjoy each other's company, or the communication just doesn't work. It is a very hard thing to realize what is happening and to take the steps to accommodate the changes in one's life. There are regrets and feelings that perhaps one has done the wrong thing. You must be aware that once you have opened your conscious mind to the truth of spiritual knowledge, it cannot be closed again. It will always be there. You can put it away for awhile in order to submit to the needs of others, but the Light within will always be pleading to be acknowledged and used.

Changes

When a soul entity finally opens its eyes to what it truly is and will be in the present lifetime, when it leaves behind what will not follow and extends its being and thoughts to others who have started on the Path of Light, the sadness will fall away to be replaced with a wonderful feeling of happiness and love. Then the soul will know it has finally found its place in the world. Then one can truly work to help others learn to come to the Light. A truly effective teacher has to have the knowledge and sureness of purpose to teach others. The Light within the teacher will shine out and pull the students to the teacher's presence and learning will begin.

Being "different" has always been a difficult situation in the world of matter; one seems to be on the edge of things, not accepted by those who set the standards. But standards are rapidly changing in your world. The truth that we are and have always been spiritual beings is beginning to be acknowledged and understood. You will find more people looking up to you with respect than with suspicion or intolerance. All around you are new ways of looking at the universe and things unseen.

Scientists are discovering universal energy; machines are being invented that can measure electrical flows around human beings, called auras, that the seers have always known existed and so on. There is little reason anymore to hide your feelings or beliefs. Now is the time to reach out to others and share with them what is happening. Send your love to others and intuit their needs in order to help them. Do not press knowledge on those who reject it, but merely sow a few seeds of knowledge that may eventually take root, even in the most stony soil.

Know that your guardian angels and spiritual teachers are constantly trying to help you. The Father of All answers your prayers through them and wants you back within His Very Being. Expect to receive, and you shall receive. Love is always there, even if you do not perceive or accept it. Receive it into yourself when you are down or depressed; it will raise your spirits to a higher level. Ask for clarity and it will come. Give your love and charity to others and it will be returned to you many times over. You know these things. We repeat them over and over again so that none can forget.

Sent with love

The Golden Path

CHAPTER FOURTEEN

The Ten Etheric Bodies

By Master Teacher Peter
1991

The First Etheric Body

Before the created soul was allowed to incarnate into matter, the Creator of All saw fit to expand the vibrations of all souls to include several extra "layers" of vibrational being. These were given so that when the soul entered a body of matter, even a nonhuman body, the perfect pattern of that body would always exist around it and that whatever injury might befall the body, the pattern would exist for the healing forces to adhere to.

The body itself is the greatest healing force. All created animals — insects, fish, mammals — have the ability to renew their own bodies. Humanity has yet to fully realize this ability, but it does reside in the cellular structure. Yes, even to the regrowth of a new limb. This is possible because of the etheric pattern surrounding the body. Even if an arm or leg has been separated from the body, the etheric limb is still there in all its perfections, giving the perfect pattern for regrowth.

The ability to grow a new limb, inner organ, bone, muscles and so on is restricted only by the human mind, which has not developed to a point of understanding that a spiritual being encased in a human body commands and directs the operation of that body in its entirety. At present, the commands of the inhabitant operate mostly through the subconscious, which orders the cells of the body to cooperate in the myriad functions that cause the body to move, feel, see, hear and be able to communicate with each other.

Gradually, mankind is beginning to learn to use its senses to regain close contacts with the Spiritual Kingdom and, because of using that ability, is now tapping into long-forgotten gifts from the Creator. Self-healing of a damaged body is being learned, but the extent to which this can be extended is still undreamed of. Humanity still believes that each person has only so many years to live in one lifetime. Today, that life has extended from about 30 or 40 years to close to 100 years.

The human body was created to last as long as the inhabitant wishes it to last – an indefinite period!

The question has been asked about how alcohol and drugs affect the etheric body. The etheric body stands alone in its perfect pattern and is not affected by such addictions. It is the physical body that is affected because unnatural addictions to foreign substances cause the conscious mind to limit the energy inflow from the etheric when the body is under the influence of such substances. When this inflow of energy is restricted for a long period of time, the first thing to suffer is the brain, and cells begin to die because of the lack of sufficient energy to renew them naturally. Without the natural energy inflow, the oxygen needed for the brain to function normally is not drawn into the body and all cells of the body suffer, as well as those in the brain. Physical cells, especially around the face, become altered and many people who constantly take these substances into their bodies experience a change in appearance as a result. The body becomes unable to renew the cells according to the etheric pattern because the energies of that pattern are being restricted. This makes us very sad to see people misuse their bodies in this manner.

As people learn how to maintain and renew this mechanism properly, the spiritual being can stay on your planet to learn and achieve as long as it desires. Your Bible gives instances of people who lived several hundred years, which has always seemed highly improbable to you, but the accounts are true. These people were those who had retained their spiritual knowledge of regrowth. They left the bodies behind only when their work was done and they wished to return to their spiritual home. People were closer in their minds to the Spiritual Kingdom in those days.

Not only will you be able to repair and renew your own bodies, but the ability to raise your human vibratory frequency is also a built-in attribute. As the mind begins to reach new heights of spiritual understanding, the body will follow suit, the cellular structure becoming finer and lighter.

The etheric body functions not only as a body pattern, but also as an indicator of the state of the body and mind. It is the etheric body that transmits this state as electrical emanations, seen to some as auras. The etheric envelope also receives and transmits to the body the universal energy that all matter consists of, acting as the regulator of the energy, allowing entrance of the exact amounts of energy required by the body and mind at any one time. It is at this point that the conscious mind also acts as a regulator of this energy. The conscious mind, when it is depressed, in a bad mood, angry or thinking spiteful thoughts (as examples) sends the signal to the etheric envelope that it does not want good, fresh energy, so that energy is withheld and stored in the etheric until called for. That is the reason for the listlessness that accompanies such emotions. When intense anger or a screaming jag is over, the energy is lacking to replace what has been badly used up.

Such inconsistencies in the emotions are part of the reason mankind has advanced so slowly in its understanding of its own spiritual nature. When it learns the fallacy of anger, the uselessness of greed, the false faces of fear, the Light of Knowledge will once again flood the minds of mankind, and the planned evolution of mankind will transform life to a new world of peace and happiness.

God bless you.

The Second Etheric Body

Many writers receiving information from spirit have named the different spiritual bodies by different terms, so, for simplicity's sake, I will number them from one to ten. Yes, there are ten spiritual bodies that emanate out from the human body and all have a very distinct relationship, both to the body and to the spiritual being that resides within it.

The second etheric body contains an essence of the Earthly vibrations that surround the human body. It is a grounding force that receives the vibrations from the first etheric body and relates the emotions and vibrations of an Earthly nature to those of higher vibrations. You must realize that vibrations created by the workings of the spiritual higher self through the physical mind and body are very strong and they project themselves outward to produce effects upon other vibrations encased in matter and those which are available to be materialized. This effect spreads like a pebble's ripples in a universal pond, especially in the third dimension. These vibrations imprint themselves upon the Akashic Records forever.

The role of the second etheric body is to filter out third-dimensional vibrations so that higher spiritual vibrations may be released into the higher etheric bodies.

Remember, all vibrations are continuously in motion in the universe. Thoughts of the soul originate on higher planes of reality, then are focused into the personality, then to the higher self of that personality to be used as guidance for the embodied personality. Those thought vibrations do not meet a dead end at that point but must continue to travel. As they are used and felt by the human mind, they then pass out through the human body into the first etheric body, having expressed mind and body. They are seen, then, as the human aura and those with the ability to see them can gain much information about that personality.

The thought vibration continues its motion into the second etheric body which absorbs the many different vibrations, clarifies the negative vibrations emanating from the aura and separates those vibrations which must remain to circulate in the third dimension. The higher, spiritual vibrations are then sent on to the third etheric body, which we will study in the next lesson.

This is also a healing level for thought vibrations that have passed through the third-dimensional time frame. Even the spiritual vibrations have been slightly altered and distorted by the experience and need to be restored to a purer consistency. Alteration of the concepts of time have to be restored to universal time, and shocks the pure spiritual vibrations suffer during the human lifetime have to be soothed and deleted before they can travel further upward toward their true level of being. It is like a huge, gentle hand, smoothing the wrinkles out of a piece of old, used fabric.

How long does this take? An instant of eternal time; a matching amount of time for the emotional vibrations as they occur in your time. It is an ongoing and constant filtering system, unaffected by the human mind or third-dimensional occurrences. It is the Hand of the Creator, recreating and restoring the personal vibrations of His children so that their eternal pattern of life will never be interrupted. This, in essence, is the function that maintains eternal life. The spiritual consciousness then continues its journey back through the soul's higher self, purified and ready to take on more experiences within the human mind and body. The Creator cares for His children.

God bless you all.

The Third Etheric Body

The third etheric body is an energy field that has the ability to protect the human body from outside radiation at levels prescribed by the Creator to be received by the Earth. Today, however, mankind has damaged the outer layers of the atmosphere to the point where more radiation is reaching humanity that was intended. The shield that God made for the body is not able to protect the body from all of this unnatural radiation, though it does filter out much of it.

When a person deliberately lies out in the sun, especially on a beach near an ocean, lake or river, the intense reflection of the sun upon the water increases the amount of radiation that the body receives. Mankind must come to realize that vanity foolishly creates the hazards of cancerous growths within the body, which this kind of radiation will increasingly promote. Your scientists have finally found just how much damage is being done and, worldwide, there is real concern about this. It will take many years after the damaging gases have ceased to rise into the atmosphere before the "holes" in the protective layers of atmosphere will return to their normal function.

The third etheric body has a second function and that is to be the receptacle for the universal energy that you exist in. All matter exists as universal energy and becomes material when thought exists to create a material being or thing. The human body is activated by this universal energy when it is conceived and as it grows within the mother's womb. The life force of the soul then enters it at birth, or shortly before birth, to make it a living, sentient being. Energy to run this human vehicle is absorbed from the "ocean" of energy around you through the third etheric body in direct proportion to the needs of the body at any given time. When the body is ill, the ratio of energy being absorbed lessens slightly as the first and second bodies have areas that are not flowing normally. All etheric bodies must flow in a normal energy pattern for the human body to be in top condition.

A healer who has the ability to see the "black holes" in a person's aura knows where to direct universal energy to correct the condition. The ability to heal is given by the Lord to lessen the effects of the Earth's environment and the accompanying ills that arise from it. The healer has the ability to draw universal energy in to the body, then focus the energy directly to the affected area of the aura. This act of focusing increases the normal energy flow to the extent that the body can then begin to correct the imbalances caused by outside bacteria or other factors.

In the case of illnesses caused by the wrong thinking of the afflicted person, and there are many, the healer can also direct universal energy to focus on the problem and the body can then balance itself. But if the thinking patterns of the person remain the same, the same condition will return.

So, the third etheric body can be thought of as a protective layer of energy with a spongy consistency that absorbs universal energy and transmits it through the first and second etheric bodies to provide the "fuel of life" for the human body.

The Fourth Etheric Body

The fourth etheric body is a vibration of sensitivity. When it comes into contact with another living being, it is this layer of being that "feels" the vibratory frequencies of the other. To those who are able to visually comprehend different auras or layers around the body, the fourth etheric body appears as the bright pulsing edge of the aura, always in motion and always seeking out frequencies around the entity. This vibration is the front line of the sense of touch in the body. It sends its minute vibrations to the tiny nerve endings on the skin and from there travels through the nervous system to the brain where the sensation is interpreted.

Long before the human body was created, this sense was part of the first spiritual beings who had intensified their vibrations in order to explore your world. It was a very necessary vibration to guide them through the fields of matter because their spiritual senses had necessarily dimmed a bit. As each succeeding progressive move into matter was implemented, this sense of touch or feeling became an even more important part of the solidified bodies. To primitive peoples who inhabited the Earth so long ago, it was extremely strong. They could sense the presence of another living being from quite a distance, enabling them to hide from danger or locate meat. Even now, the hair on your body will sometimes rise when you sense danger nearby. This is the strong impulse of the fourth etheric body sending a very intense vibration to the body.

As your mental sensitivity increases during these wonderful times of change, so will the strength of the fourth etheric body. The higher self directs the etheric bodies and manipulates them according to the needs of the embodied soul. The sense of touch and the ability to feel vibrations will become very important to the survival of the human race in the next one hundred years. For a long time, the phenomenon of ESP has been quite widespread and talked about. This sensing through the reception of vibrations from the fourth etheric body is already being used when the conscious mind accepts incoming impulses and recognizes them for what they are. As this knowledge increases in mankind, a person could easily roam through complete darkness without seeing with his eyes at all.

Those of you who are blind are already using this ability to find your way about quite well and, as time passes, the ability to sense what is around you will become highly focused; blindness will not be a disability at all.

The sensing process can be heightened by consciously thinking about that pulsing "feeler" you have and reaching out with your mind to strengthen it. Learn to feel with your mind what is around you. That vibrational direction-finder is always there, but few realize it or really try to use it. At night, practice sensing what is in front of you or beside you without using your hands. It will not take long before you will know there is something solid there. When you realize this and reach out to touch it, take note of how far away from your body the object is. This is the distance your fourth etheric body operates from your body.

When your senses are well developed in this way, you will notice that your closed eyes will produce impressions of what is there. The eyes naturally bring pictures of what you see through optic nerves to the brain, but when the eyes are inactive and the conscious mind is receiving the vibrations accurately from the fourth etheric body, a picture of the object will be translated into form within the mind. You may find that concept a bit far-fetched, but remember, those in the spirit do not have material eyes; all is sensed from vibrations on all frequency levels. Again, the blind have the opportunity to reach this level of understanding far sooner that the rest of humanity. It just takes a great deal of concentration and practice.

This is the last etheric body that can be seen by the human body with the eyes. The others may be sensed only by the higher spiritual probing of the developed conscious mind or by the connection to the higher self.

My blessings to you all.

The Fifth Etheric Body

Outside the range of conscious seeing is a band of vibration known as the fifth etheric body. This is also a pulsing frequency that is a conductor of creative energy from universal energy that flows all about the embodied entity. The human body, as you know, creates new cells all the time. Cells that die are cast off into the system of elimination within the body. In order to provide conscious tissue for the new cells being created, the fifth etheric body is constantly absorbing the nuclei for such cells and directing them into the body where they are gathered and coalesced by the subconscious mind into new cells.

The subconscious mind is more than you believe it to be. It is that part of the soul mind that has the God-given knowledge of the pattern of the human body and it is assigned the job of building and maintaining that pattern to keep the body functioning properly. The fuel it needs is provided by food and drink the body takes in and by energy elements fed to it by the fifth etheric body.

Constant streams of creative energy are drawn to any life form in the universe and are always most active near those forms. All of the most minute particles of energy have a form of consciousness and are a part of the Creator who formed them. In order for matter to appear at all, each particle must understand how it is to join with others in order to form anything to be created into matter. Each particle obeys the direction of God, so it must have that conscious mind, so to speak. All cells in a human body have enough consciousness to be able to fit the pattern of that body and function correctly. All cellular structures that are directed by God to form a certain living or inert being or thing are directed into the pattern of that created being or thing and, in order that the creation is perfect to its pattern, all cells contain the entire pattern. That way, if some cells are too weak or not able to complete their job, other cells may step in and take their place. This is the holographic structure you have been hearing about.

If cells in the brain of a human being are damaged or killed, there are generally other cells that can do the job once the personality is trained to use them. This is called redirecting. How else could these other brain cells take on the new directives if they were not aware of all functions of the brain? If your surgeons were to take cells from a leg and transplant them into the brain, the cells would still be able to function as brain cells because each of them has the entire pattern of the body instilled within it. Patterns of the Infinite Creator have left nothing to chance. Creation is perfect and the intended patterns for each human being are perfect, according to the intent of the soul being who is to inhabit them. When a body is born with imperfections that cause it to be crippled in mind or body, this is still the perfect pattern intended by the soul being before birth. If, during the lifetime of the soul being, changes are to be made, they are made with the permission of the higher self and the pattern can be changed.

Just as each cell and each particle of energy are holistic in nature, so each etheric body also contains the full knowledge of the function of the others. If any frequency is disturbed for any reason, the function of that etheric body is assumed by another. All creation is interconnected. All is one.

Bless you this day.

The Sixth Etheric Body

This etheric body is a frequency of light and through it are transmitted the color rays of being. There are many spectrums of light in the universe that are perceived by humanity and many that are not. For this reason, we will consider only seven of them.

The sixth etheric body acts as both a conductor and a filter for these color rays so that the higher frequencies too strong for your bodies are not permitted to be harmful. As your minds and bodies evolve, more of these color rays will be opened to your consciousness and used according to their benefits.

The color spectrum that you deal with has been set into place in the rainbow you see in the atmosphere and in light that filters through crystals from the light of the Sun. Each color transmits certain properties of love and emotions which simply translate into the many facets of the love of God. There are many studies being sent regarding these rays, so I will not go into them at this time.

Sunlight that you receive on your body is a most important element for life in your dimension. The spectrum of color rays it imparts to you is every bit as important as the life-giving energy that fuels your universe. Being aware of this fact enables your body and consciousness to absorb the color rays even better than if you were unaware. It is well to spend a few minutes in the morning sun every day, as that is the time when the color rays are projecting toward you at an angle. The angle of the rays has a great deal to do with the body's assimilation of them. When the Sun has just come over your horizon and is hitting the Earth for the first time in a day, that is the best time to stand in its rays.

Color rays are not limited by physical sight, however, and the conscious mind can call them in at any time by clearing the mind and concentrating upon the color ray that is wished. Although the rays are a part of the Sun's magnificent solar powers, they are also an active creation of God, created to be used by all life forms for their spiritual upliftment and happiness. Either way of receiving them is most beneficial to the soul entity.

The sixth etheric body is a vital, living frequency that serves to enhance your life and to protect you from higher frequencies you are not ready for as yet. As your awareness grows and your conscious thoughts evolve toward a higher plane, your sixth etheric body will allow higher frequencies of the color rays to penetrate the human body to give you the added benefit of their universal powers.

We are with you always.

The Seventh Etheric Body

As vibrational emanations spread out from the body, they do not become lighter, but instead become denser. Etheric bodies have very important functions, for both the physical body and the spiritual body. This is a learning period for the spiritual being and experiences in the material world are very important to its education.

Whenever there are events that create traumas to the physical body or mind, they are absorbed and acted upon by the seventh etheric body, which acts as a buffer to the spiritual being. The sensitivity of the spiritual being is highly developed and worldly traumas are very difficult for those higher vibrations to withstand at the third-dimensional level. It is for that reason that a buffer zone was needed for protection.

Do not misunderstand; traumatic events to be encountered during an incarnation are very important for the spiritual entity to experience. It is for that reason that it has incarnated. In the lifetime to be lived in the third dimension, there are trials and errors that must be encountered, dealt with and learned from. During these encounters, severe injury to the body or to the mind often happens. The spiritual entity must be able to experience these events more objectively than the human mind in order to help the human mind deal with the situation. The buffer of the seventh etheric body absorbs the trauma only to the extent of taking the sharp edges off, so to speak.

In turn, the spiritual entity, or higher self, is then able to act as a buffer, counselor and guide to the human mind for the solution to the problem or the ability to cope with trauma in a way that will give the human mind the chance to meet the challenge successfully. Of course, if that mind has not opened itself to the guidance from within, such traumas are that much more difficult.

The seventh etheric body also acts as a buffer zone for harmful bacteria that surround the human body at all times. If all the potential infections that are constantly around reached the human body, there would be little chance of survival. Those that are allowed to penetrate the etheric bodies do so by the acceptance of the spiritual entity for the learning situations the entity must go through. Illness of the body comes for many reasons. If the human mind dwells on the subject of illness, it draws that bacteria through the barriers created by God. The higher self knows that the experience of illness is important for its own learning and that the human mind, whether asking for guidance or not, needs to understand its own role in the prevention and healing of the body. Healing cannot be learned when there is no reason for it.

When the human mind, acting with the higher self, realizes the very active role it can take in self-healing, it becomes a partner with the seventh etheric body in that it is rejecting the bacteria, rejecting incorrect movements within the body and seeing the body corresponding to the perfect pattern created for it. To understand the functions of all of the spiritual bodies that make up life in the spiritual world, as well as the in material world, is an important part of the evolvement of mankind.

We send you our love and blessings.

The Eighth Etheric Body

The eighth etheric body holds a special factor for the protection of mankind. It is a band of violet light which stores energy from the Sun for the use of the body when the Sun is obscured by clouds. This is a different energy from that which penetrates all etheric bodies and pours into the human body at all times. That is universal energy, the very being of the Creator.

Energy coming from your Sun holds many different rays that are very important for life on your planet, yet that energy can be dangerous if it reaches the body in amounts that the body cannot deal with effectively at one time. The eighth etheric body cannot store enormous amounts of this radiation if the human being insists on staying too long in the Sun's rays. It can and does, however, retain a great deal of it, and maintains a "storage vault" of energy for the body when the rays have been withheld from the body for too long. If the period without exposure to the Sun is too long, then the storage vault is depleted and the human body begins to suffer from lack of essential elements of the Sun.

Currently, radiation from the Sun is hitting the Earth in amounts that pose dangers to humanity to some degree and, if solutions are not found in the next few years, protection from the Sun's rays will have to be found. This creates the problem of getting necessary exposure for the body to remain balanced and yet protecting against too much. For each person, there are essential amounts that are needed and they vary greatly. The importance of being in touch with the higher self becomes greater as time goes on, for knowledge of what is needed for each body to be entirely accurate must be obtained from that source. Sun creams that are produced to filter out dangerous rays are available now and should be used, if at all possible. If the expense is too great, use oils processed from sunflower seed. There is a natural protectorant there.

If gaps in the protective atmospheric layer become larger and spread around the world, protection will be necessary also for plants that supply food. Dangerous radiation can damage cells in grains, fruits and vegetables which, in turn, can damage cells in the human body.

Sun bathing in your present time is foolhardy. The surface of the skin is an extremely important part of the body and needs to be cared for with intelligence and gentleness. That means protective clothing should be worn, covering as much of the body as possible during long periods of exposure to the Sun. Light cotton cloth will protect from damaging rays, yet will be comfortable even in very hot weather. Heavy tanning of the skin restricts skin cells from breathing effectively by not providing the cells with the necessary openings for the energy the body needs.

Why be so concerned with the color of the skin? Each human has the color of skin that is necessary in the formation of his or her body. That color is important for the proper balance of the body. Glory in your own color and take care of your skin.

The Ninth Etheric Body

To compensate for the physical body's lack of purpose without the presence of a spiritual entity within, the ninth etheric body is a layer of energy that seals the spiritual entity into the body. You might liken it to a beautiful wrapping on an important gift that has been given to humanity.

This layer of energy also acts as a deterrent to the soul entity from changing its mind and withdrawing from the body too rapidly. This does happen, of course, but unless that has been determined from the beginning, as in the case of withdrawal from a baby's body for karmic reasons, it is not easy. The Creator makes it quite clear to those making decisions to incarnate into flesh that it is a decision not to be made lightly. Once the decision is made, that lifetime must be lived.

There are very few human beings who advance far enough on their Path to Light that they are able to blend with their higher self to the extent that the decision to leave the body can be made consciously. The few who can accomplish that feat seldom do, for they realize that lessons must be learned and coped with before the spiritual self has the right to leave.

To occupy a human body is a great responsibility, not only to the soul entity making that decision, but to all those with whom it will share that lifetime. The concept of karma is extremely complicated, so much so that the human mind will never completely be able to untangle the interwoven web of circumstances and interrelationships that are involved. When a soul entity enters a human body, whether by birth or by taking over an adult body with its spiritual consent, it enters this web and becomes a part of it. This is the greater responsibility: to work through all of the events that dictate the harmony of that karmic net.

During all the centuries mankind has dwelled upon your planet, only a handful of soul entities have declined to stay with the lifetime they chose, breaking through the ninth etheric body in anger or frustration and returning to the Spiritual Kingdom. They return in disgrace and are required to start all over again on their own paths. They were not ready for the learning they tried to take on themselves and the loving Father starts their re-education.

We know that the life you have undertaken can often be very hard, with frustrations, grief and traumas all around. But be very aware that every time these emotional and physical difficulties are coped with successfully and overcome, there is rejoicing in the spiritual realm, for you have stepped up a rung on the ladder to the ultimate Light of God. This is why you are here. Wringing the hands and blaming fate and/or everyone else will not solve problems or overcome twisted emotions. Only inner determination to work toward solutions will make the difference between being beaten down and succeeding.

You know you are not alone. You have the love and strength of many spiritual beings, all working under the direction of the Almighty Creator, ready and willing to help you, guide and protect you whenever you ask. When you open to this loving help and watch the little miracles that happen every day, there can be no denying that heavenly connection. Use it and you will be able to succeed in your purpose for incarnating, no matter what the deterrents. You are the Wondrous Children of God; nothing can stand in your way but your own stubborn free will. You are giants of strength if you will only recognize your own stature!

We send you our love and guidance.

The Tenth Etheric Body

Picture now the human body standing alone, with all of the energetic layers of Light pulsing around it. The very outer layer glows with a shining white Light, for it is the tenth etheric body that proclaims to all other entities in the vast conclaves of space that this being is a Child of God, to be respected as such!

The outer layer of shining energy is the connection between the spiritual entity, the human body and God. It is actually part of the Eternal One, His sign upon you that you belong to Him forever. It is that part of you that is a part of God.

This knowledge has not been given to mankind before. It is the forerunner of much new knowledge that is now coming into the upper ethers of your planet, and that will have to do with new understanding of yourselves and your spiritual being, new technical knowledge and knowledge of your universe and the many more universes that exist beyond your present scope of awareness.

Energies that exist around your world today are enabling the mind of humanity to expand to a degree never before even imagined. Open wide your minds and receive what the Eternal One is offering to you.

The blessings of the Creator and all created beings are surrounding you even now. Feel them and be thankful.

CHAPTER FIFTEEN

Chakras

By Master Teacher Hilarian
1993

Now that you have had an overview of the etheric bodies, it is important that we set out some information about the chakra system.

"Chakra" is, again, an Eastern word that has no English counterpart. It describes energy systems placed in the body that act as swirling, highly concentrated intakes of universal energy likened to seven electrical generators all working at once, but powered by that universal energy instead of gasoline. These "generators" serve to keep the important parts of the body highly energized and activated at all times. They are the means by which energy is kept moving through the body. This activation of energy in the sixth and seventh chakras provides the powerful means by which a human being is motivated to use energy to connect with the higher self and other higher-dimensional forces.

Sensitive persons who are able to see auras can also see the whirling colors of the body chakras, which enables a healer to detect any chakra system that is not functioning properly.

There are many, many good books delving very deeply into the chakra systems, which we sincerely hope you will take the time to obtain and study. The energy systems that control your body are your real connection to the underlying life force of the universe, from where you were created. Briefly, they are the following:

The first chakra, which lies at the bottom of the spine, governs the most basic energy of the body, controls strength, decision-making and the motivation to progress. It is here that fear finds a physical response. This was the first chakra to develop in mankind, for it fueled the response to danger and the basic instinct to survive. The energy here is seen as the color red.

The second chakra is located between the first chakra and the navel and is the center of the sexual drive and of creativity. Stress and disharmony tend to freeze up the elimination process of the body, but if conscious attention is focused upon the second chakra area, this can be overcome and straightened out by additional energy being pulled in at that point. This energy system is seen as the color orange.

The third chakra lies between the second chakra and the rib cage, and is known as the solar plexus chakra. Many call this the "seat of the soul" because it is at the center of the body. When you read material telling you to "center" yourself, this is where the mental focus should be. This is where the feelings of strength and determination spring from; this is where peace finds its home. There is where all emotions originate. The color here is yellow.

The fourth chakra is the heart chakra, located, of course, in the heart area of the body. The is the center of spiritual love, physical love and of the feelings you have of good and evil. Here is where spiritual guidance finds its response in what you call the conscience. When you have done something wrong for you or for others, here is where the deep heavy feeling sets in. When there are feelings of great joy, you feel as though your heart could burst with joy! How many times have you heard that? Life in the physical body is the most alive here in this great chakra and those who listen carefully to its messages find life abounding with good health and close communication with themselves. No, its color is not red, it is green —the color of healing. Where do the feelings of compassion and love originate? The heart chakra.

The fifth chakra lies in the throat, just below the vocal chords. Energy here works to help you communicate with yourself and others. It provides the strength and courage to speak out of your own knowledge and seek the knowledge of others. The "lump in the throat" is caused by mental blockage of the energy of the fifth chakra. Its color is blue.

The sixth chakra is centered at your forehead, between your brows and a little above. This is what is called the third eye chakra, for it connects to the pineal gland deep in your brain, which is the seat of spiritual knowledge. During meditation, if attention is focused at this point, you will feel deep responses in your mind from the Spiritual Kingdom. How to open this third eye is explained in another chapter. Be aware of this most important energy center, for it is the pathway to higher knowledge. Occasionally, when someone has a head injury, this gland is stimulated and the person immediately becomes aware of the thoughts of others, is able to see into the future, etc. This knowledge can be obtained through deep meditation. Its color is indigo.

The seventh chakra is located at the top of the head where the bones grew together after birth. The energy that is absorbed at this point is the highly spiritual energy of the soul which provides your connection to the higher self. It activates the human mind and protects it from the negative vibrations which abound in your world. It is also a powerful energy intake for the entire body when you are aware that it can be. Healers focus on bringing in this energy on the intake of breath, pulling in down into the body while exhaling. When this is done in a time of meditation, it will bring powerful energies to work with. Its color is violet.

There are other, higher chakras that are spiritual in nature, but that we will not go into at this point.

You are beginning to understand that the body is not a simple machine composed of parts and pieces. It is a finely tuned mechanism, created by God, directed by the subconscious, fueled by universal energy and activated by the life force of your true spiritual being. By focusing on individual chakras during meditation, even a very light meditation, you can increase the energy flow to your mind and body through that chakra.

Try to bring all these concepts together and see your body in a different way. Every human being has the responsibility to care for this miraculous piece of vibrating matter. Putting your body into dangerous situations on purpose simply to obtain a thrill is like thumbing your nose at the Creator. Being able to incarnate at all at this time of great changes is a great privilege and challenge. Use this lifetime wisely and gratefully.

The Golden Path

CHAPTER SIXTEEN

The Dark Forces and Love

By Master Teacher Peter
1990

In this Turning Time, the dark forces are extremely busy, using their influence to turn man's mind from the Light into darkness in order to gain new and powerful energies for themselves. The dark forces are present in the world and ever have been, having been born of Lucifer's battle against his Creator. Lucifer has now repented, been reborn and is on his way to the Light, but the ideas he created have never left the universe and live on in multitudes of the higher dimensions and in millions of those incarnated to human form. It is not hard to know who they are, but the dark forces exist in many who are completely unaware of their presence and they wait to take over the emotions and minds of their hosts.

Religions in general have always taught this in a sense, and it is wrong for the proponents of the "New Age" to say that there is no such thing. They exist. And they must be dealt with by every individual incarnated in human form. The sudden unexplained surges of anger, the desire to "get back" at someone, the need to be better than someone else, the greed, the overstated sexual desires are all manifestations of the dark forces within mankind. Those on the road to enlightenment are no strangers to them and are aware of their frightening power even more because of the sensitivity acquired on the path.

Pushing these feelings down inside is not the answer. They must be dealt with on the conscious level by looking at them realistically, knowing them for what they are and, with all one's strength, surrounding them with love, thus transforming the negative feelings to positive ones, or love. Only love, the Essence of God, the Creation, the life force energy can negate the dark forces that infest mankind. This has always been known but seldom realized and worked with on a determined, conscious level. That is what has to be done at this time. For do not doubt it, what is coming to mankind in the next few decades will demand all of the physical and spiritual strength that mankind can command in order to survive and set up a new order of civilization under the total rule of the Christ. Those who do not fight the dark forces but let themselves be overtaken will have failed their test on Earth. They will then be sent to other dimensions where they will have to start their climb again up the stairway of experience and knowledge.

How to deal with those of the dark forces that are in people around you? Again, with love. Speak softly and knowingly. If you are injured by them, know that your injury is only of the body, that the person who injured you has been injured in a far greater manner. Seek to say words to them that will find a crack in which you can sow a seed that will grow and overcome the wall of discord and darkness within their awareness.

Words are powerful weapons against the dark forces. Many excellent books have been and are being written now to awaken the interest and hidden knowledge within each being to see once again the truth that awaits. Each writer aspires to a given way of presenting his or her truth and knowledge and, for every writer, there is a reader who can respond to that certain style. Search for the truth within, without in the teachings of others, in well-written books that explain what you are trying to learn. We are sending the message in every way we can.

Blend your consciousness with your inner truth and let it see the Light; do not hold it inside, hugging it to you in secret. Each being is one with all atoms, with all spiritual beings, with all physical beings, with all animal manifestations, with all nature. Put yourselves back into nature where you can feel that oneness in life. As they say, go hug a tree and feel the life force within it. Press freshly opened flowers to your face; lie in the grass; wade in flowing waters. Open yourselves to God in all these things and you will feel an opening within and wish to share it by outpouring everything you feel to the whole world!

Love is sharing, an open, beautiful burst of creative energy that cannot be held within. Love that is hoarded and kept within oneself is not real love; it is a greedy grasping that will only feed the dark forces that are just waiting for stagnant energy. Love must flow in and out of our beings like a swiftly flowing stream, which freshens itself by that flow over the rocks and weeds of life, ever renewing its energy by that wondrous movement. The life force energy itself is in constant flow in the universe. Every atom and piece of energy is in constant motion. To restrict the flow in the universe or in one's life is to create death and darkness.

Let your thoughts flow; open your inner mind to communication from your own higher self and to those in higher dimensions who are trying to educate you on this plane of experience. Keep your imagination active; create new thoughts and ideas; be aware of the needs of others and think of ways in which you can be of help. Keep your body in motion and in good repair in order to keep your mind at active attention.

Send out loving thoughts to others; they feel them. Restrict unloving thoughts and surround them with love. Give your hand to the stranger and send love energy to that person; he or she will feel it and be drawn to you. Touching others is not a suspiciously sexual thing to do, but should be a sharing of love and energy from one to another. It is natural to put an arm around people who are in pain or grieving. This has been given as a natural reaction for you to give that loving energy to help them in their hour of trauma. Be not held back by some of today's restrictions set by the dark forces. Human beings need each others' energies; they need to share with another that warm feeling of love, however briefly given.

When you shake hands, hold the grip a little longer and mean it; it will be felt. When you touch another's shoulder, leave your hand there a little longer and send love energies through that touch to the person; it will be felt and appreciated. A kiss on the cheek, even a peck, is a powerful expression of love, if given in love. Reach out to each other; love each other. Weave a web of love and sharing around all you know and the dark forces are defeated.

Given with love

The Golden Path

CHAPTER SEVENTEEN

Opening the Third Eye

By Master Teacher Marian
1991

T his is the one who walks in the Light. You may call me Marian. My focus is, perhaps, a little more feminine than the others who inhabit this dimension.

My message is focused toward the opening of the third eye in mankind. Learning to use the abilities that one has learned through all incarnations in spirit and in matter is extremely important today. Having these so-called psychic abilities will enable those who have developed them to see and understand more fully and deeply the knowledge that is now being sent to your planet. The mind of a human was given a veil at birth so that the learning process could be an easy and gradual one. The pineal gland was placed in the brain to implement that veil, but now it should be activated.

Of course, there are many people who penetrate that veil at an early age and have learned to use it either wisely and for the benefit of mankind or simply as a method to glorify their own greed. It is better that spiritual wisdom be born again into mankind before the veil is parted.

How to do this? Depending upon karmic patterns still to be worked out or learned, most people can accomplish it. The only pathway to the third eye is through deep meditation. Even if one has practiced that form of personal worship and enlightenment, it can take a long time to focus the inner energy well enough to accomplish the goal of total knowingness.

Penetrating the intense vibrations that really compose the gland cannot happen all at once, for this would "blow you away"! The abilities and knowledge that are blocked by this tiny organ are far beyond what the human mind can really conceive of. The first indications that you have successfully touched and knocked at that door will be unexpected psychic experiences, sudden flashes of insight and foreknowledge of small events. Use each ability as it comes, fully accepting and welcoming it. *Keep them to yourself as much as possible, for you will still be learning to use them in wisdom.* Psychic knowledge will be a wonderful tool for those of you who teach and heal, for you will be able to gain valuable insights into the lives of others you are trying to help. Again, keep the knowledge to yourself, for you would then have the responsibility of carrying personal knowledge that, in many cases, your friend or client would not want revealed. Use it wisely, only for *their* benefit.

It is important to realize that impressions of the unseen, visions of things to come, and so on, are not always those things you might wish to see. Dipping into the future can give knowledge of horrendous events that will frighten you or make you want to do something to prevent what is being seen. Yes, the future can be changed to some extent and there may be times when something you can do might be able to change a disastrous event. This is where wisdom comes in — the wisdom to understand what can be changed and what cannot. Generally, you will have to stand aside and wait for the event to occur in its own time. It is rare that such a vision will come with a computer-like time and date line printed across it, which makes it almost impossible to know when it will happen. Our Creator put that little feature in so that His created souls would not be able to mess with things that did not concern them.

Using inner abilities is a great responsibility to those who succeed in parting the veil of knowledge. It is not to be used as a source of income on a commercial basis (although receiving compensation for teaching or healing falls into the category of a "worker receiving proper pay").

Now, how to focus the mind to open the third eye. While in a deep state of meditation, gradually shift your focus to the forehead between the eyebrows. When a strong feeling of pressure is felt there, begin to move it inward to the center of your brain. This takes some practice. Concentrate the focus of energy strongly and evenly, directing, with your mind, that the storehouse of knowledge be opened to you. You might repeat over and over again the word "open," or whatever word seems appropriate.

Try to hold that focus for at least five minutes.

Doing this once a day over a period of time will bring a new outlook on your life and the lives of others. You will begin to see things from a different point of view and be able to use this knowledge to make life a little easier. Again, accept what you see, feel or hear. At first, you may think it is imagination, but it is not; it is your own spiritual abilities and knowledge that are beginning to be reborn. To keep a watchful eye on your progress, it might be well to keep a small journal of each occurrence. You will be surprised at how often and how deeply they will affect you. Dreams have a way of getting away from us when we awaken. Many of the thoughts or visions you will receive may act in the same way at first, so it is wise to record them just as you would a dream.

There is so much for mankind to learn before this century fades away that we are anxious for all of you to be able to use all of your physical and spiritual abilities to absorb the knowledge that is being sent at this time.

Thank you for your attention. Sent with love.

The Golden Path

CHAPTER EIGHTEEN

Ascension and Illumination

By Master Teacher Sananda
1992

M any different groups of seekers have many different sets of terms or phrases for the same things. "Ascension" is a term that relates to the passage of the soul returning into the spiritual dimension whence it originated. There are some who believe that one can exist in a higher dimension at the same time as the spirit is inhabiting the body in the third dimension. This is not the way your experience in matter was designed.

Ascension can be achieved in a way by reaching such a high spiritual level while in the body that it is possible to have spiritual contacts with ease and even to visit in a higher dimension for a short time occasionally. There are not many soul entities who have that capability at your time in space, but children born within the past few years and those being born now will see such a mental and spiritual accomplishment as a normal occurrence. As the human race evolves further into the future, spiritual and mental abilities will increase to the point where the veil between the dimensions will be thin indeed.

The ascension of Christ in His glorified body into the clouds on the mount is an experience many highly spiritual people aspire to, and their lives are spent largely with this goal uppermost in their minds and everyday activities. There is nothing wrong in this if they are, at the same time, also succeeding in completing the purpose for which they came into matter. It must be realized that when the soul entity is released back into the spiritual realm after the death of the body, that will be their ultimate ascension! If one tries to blot out the features of life in the material body and live totally in the higher consciousness of deep meditation, the purpose is lost and a lifetime is wasted.

Ascension generally means that the body of the mortal becomes glorified (the vibrations of the body being raised to such a high rate that it becomes a spiritual body), and the spiritual being itself stays together with the glorified body and rises into the spiritual realms as one. Christ had a very real purpose for doing this in the sight of His disciples. He wanted them to physically see Him rise into the heavens so that there would never be any hesitation or misunderstanding about it. He had taught His followers a great deal of what they needed to know, but these people still lived in an age of little knowledge and what Christ taught them was done in a manner they could not mistake.

There is little need for a glorified body in the spiritual realm, for each soul entity automatically retains the etheric body it was given at the moment of birth into matter. This etheric pattern remains with the entity as long as it is needed. When the soul entity becomes one with the Light beings all around it again, the need to retain that body pattern evaporates.

Given a real purpose for incarnating takes a great deal of strength and desire to progress further along the Path of Life. It is not taken lightly by any soul entity. Sliding back into matter is not a pleasant thing for most soul entities, but the need to learn the lessons and to erase karmic debts is very strong. It is important that the human mind be taught and elevated to the point that it is aware of the spiritual being that dwells behind and within it. That is why we have been trying so hard to transmit as much knowledge and wisdom as possible to the human race; it is most important for the evolution of humanity. At the same time, however, humanity must spend most of its time raising the knowledge and vesting all peoples with the love of their Creator. This takes conscious wisdom, work and time. We are indeed asking you to live in two "worlds," but you alone must decide the proportions your own needs dictate.

"Illumination" is an old term, used by many religions that are aware of the spiritual being in humanity. Another term used today with the same meaning is "revelation." Basically, it is a spiritual experience that comes to an individual without warning and without being sought after. There are few seekers who do not yearn for this type of experience, but it is given to very few.

Ascension and Illumination

It comes with a flash of very bright light, and current surroundings simply fade away from the conscious mind. In their place the consciousness expands into the higher consciousness and blends with it, and the entire spiritual being keeps expanding into time and space. All things become as one and all knowledge is instantly given. The expanded spirit is instantly surrounded with the love and peace of the Creator and experiences all of the vast reaches of space and time. All is complete clarity and beauty. There is no time, no sense of anything but the infinite. It seems to go on forever, but actually it usually only lasts for just a few minutes of your time. Gradually, the expanded awareness draws back until the conscious mind returns to its human status. It is a shock and an immense disappointment. The memories of that all-knowing quickly fade away and what is left in the mind is the certainty that it did happen and that the knowledge is there somewhere, hidden in memory. The love and peace encountered remains always, and that individual will never look at his or her current lifetime in the same way again.

Why is this gift given only to a special few? There are too many variations of reasons to fully describe. For some, this experience had been arranged for that lifetime to help the entity fulfill a very important purpose. For others, there are other motives. Sometimes one who has given up, who should have done things differently, is given a new lease on that life; sometimes it is given as a reward for a life well lived. Can one obtain the experience by asking for it in prayer? You can ask, of course. It is still up to those in the spiritual realm who are guiding your way to gauge if such an experience would be beneficial to you or not.

Most spiritual experiences come without warning and are given for definite reasons. It is best to work with the life you are living now and do the best you can. Follow the teachings given in the Bible and by the master teachers who are speaking through many open channels now, and you will find the choice of paths is not that difficult. The inner wisdom of the Christ Spirit will show you the way.

Again, illumination will be yours when the doorway to the infinite is opened after the incarnation in matter is completed. It is never wrong to strive for the highest form of spirituality you can, just be sure to strike a balance. All will be clear when you re-enter your true home.

Our love for you is growing every day and the love of the Almighty Creator of All continues to expand through all universes, as creation goes on eternally.

The Golden Path

CHAPTER NINETEEN

Peace

By Master Teacher Hilarian
1991

P eace is a beautiful word that has different meanings for different people. In the sense of a world not at war, it has the connotation of people going about their daily routine without fear of being harassed or killed. A peaceful world is a world without war, a very rare happening.

Peace in that sense is a wonderful thing, but is only a kind of protective mist over humanity that is sought for. What happens under that mist? What about peace in individual governments? A body of men and women who determine the status of services for a country or city make the rules that people must live by in their constituency, who convene and speak their minds and ideas in a atmosphere of peace and understanding. Now, that would be nice. Unfortunately, peaceful inner attitudes are not usually on the agenda for most lawmakers; they are too busy balancing their own political lives with the issues at hand. No, there is no peace there.

Among the crowds of people hastily finding their way among their fellow man on congested streets and sidewalks, is peace found? Not very often. Irritation, frustration, pressure to be somewhere in time, worries about earning enough money to provide for themselves and their families — these are the feelings in the vibrations. No, there is little peace there, either.

Where, then, is the "peace beyond all understanding" that the Christ gave to humanity?

In a quiet place, whether it be a broom closet, a sunny meadow, a secluded beach, by a flowing river or a lake in the evening, it is easier to find the peace the harried person is looking for, at least for awhile. Perhaps such a time will last for a weekend or just a day. Then what? Back to the old routine and the same frustrations and worries.

Is that all there is? No.

The Peace of God resides deep within each individual, given to each spiritual being at its creation, to remain in their inner conscious structure forever. No one can give it to you; no one can take it away.

But where is it when you need it during your busy day? Right there, but it takes a little cultivation to realize it and feel it. How? Now that I have your attention, I'll tell you.

The human conscious mind was created to take care of the day-to-day events and responsibilities that are necessary in a human embodiment, and it is a marvelous instrument. A peaceful mind can be accomplished on this level, but it must first be realized on the inner level. Let's take "John," for example (a good name). From childhood he is trained and taught that he must be a real man, strong in body and mind, able to take responsibility in his life by working hard and providing for the family he will have someday. Perhaps his family was not particularly religious, so he has to rely entirely upon his own resources to achieve these things. By middle life, he has achieved position, money and a large family, which puts great burdens on his shoulders. All of his waking moments are consumed by planning, work and worries. He has lost sight of who and what he is, because there was never any time to really find out. His life has become almost mechanical. One day, he has a mild heart attack which throws him into a really frightening situation. He finally realizes that he is a person; then he wonders what kind of person? He begins to look over his life to assess how well he has done. Through all of this, there is the realization that something very vital has been missed along the way and he cannot understand what it might be.

Perhaps he then goes back to his normal life and activities, having to put aside the "crazy meanderings" of his mind during his illness. Still, there is something missing. If he is lucky, or if his spiritual guardians put something or someone in his way, someone will say something or he will read something that will make him realize that there is a wonderful something he has missed. Perhaps he will join a class or seminar on meditation, because it might help him to relax a bit. This is successful and he learns to take time out for himself and give his body and mind a small rest period during the day. Good start! Eventually, this feels so good that he starts giving himself some time at home, too, when the kids are quiet and his wife is busy with something else. One day, when deep in the quiet of spirit, there is a voice or a vision that affects him deeply. He realizes, finally, that there is more to life than what he sees and feels all the time. More and more he goes into the silence and eventually reaches that beautiful inner self that is the connection to the Supreme Intelligence that he has always denied, but now cannot.

The experience changes his life. He sees himself and all other human beings in a new light and understanding. As time goes on, the inner peace he has always had begins to be felt. What a wonderful feeling! Beneath all of the hassles of life, beneath the bickering of politicians and the horrors of war all over the globe, no matter how much pressure there is from the job is The Peace, the knowing that regardless of anything that Earth can toss at him, The Peace is there. It is the foundation for his life and nothing can change it, a foundation that is built upon the love that is God, Eternal Love. John has found the divine security that he has always searched for and will never be without again.

That foundation of peace is what gives the soul entity the strength, incentive and serenity to lead a lifetime on your planet. It is that inner peace that allows the soul entity to be aware of the guidance from the spiritual kingdom, called conscience, that helps it to fulfill the purpose for which it came into embodiment. Without the inner peace and the inner silence that goes with it, one cannot be aware of what this lifetime is all about. So many go through their lives living on a shallow saucer of hardened stone, never realizing there is something more, searching for something they cannot put a finger on. They substitute physical thrills and experiences that take all of their attention for a time. After the letdown that comes when there are no lasting effects from such "highs," they look for more, in the hope "something" will surface that will give them something wonderful.

Something wonderful does exist, but it must be searched for in the correct way.

If you have not done so already, please give yourself the priceless gift of inner silence. That silence is the entrance to your mind and heart for the spiritual beings who are trying to reach you. That silence is the way that the very atoms of energy and love that surround you and are part of God can enter and give you the inner peace that you hunger for with all of your heart and mind.

The end of an age is approaching and with it many changes will occur in your lives. Now is the time to achieve that inner peace that mankind cannot possibly fully understand, for that alone will give you the confidence and strength to go forth into that new world to come on Earth without fear or trembling. We who reside in the higher dimensions are trying endlessly to help you in any way we can. Send your prayers to the One Father of All for assistance, and we who are His devoted servants will be there to help. It is time for you to enter that state of peace. Nothing in your present life can even come close to it. It is yours; claim it again.

We send you God's Love and Peace forevermore.

CHAPTER TWENTY

Today's Relationships

By Master Teacher Peter
1990

Today's children have grown up in difficult circumstances. Parents have divorced, remarried or are just living with someone not their spouse. This is true not in the United States alone, but in many countries and cultures around the world. Society is placing so many strains on humanity that the family unit that God decreed for His children is fast dissolving. Young people are not being taught how to respect the laws of God or themselves, much less others they come in contact with. Men still see women as chattel and a wife as a servant, a permanent mistress and/or a slave. Although the Old Testament laws of society were pretty much directed that way, the Creator never meant a man/woman relationship to be like that.

In your era, women are rebelling against this kind of thinking and demanding that they be recognized for what they are, soul entities with minds and needs of their own. So where does this leave you now? The old laws of the Ten Commandments are being turned upside-down; men and women are confused about their roles in society; men and women are confused about their sexual roles; parents are upset at seeing their children floundering in this confusion and the offspring of today's matches and mismatches are suffering from what they see as abandonment by one parent or the other, or both. They are growing up without the love and security that every child should have in a family group. This is confusing them about who they are and hindering their feelings about being accepted in the world. It is a sad state of affairs.

Why is all this happening? It is a part of opening to the awareness of who you are which has been in progress for the past hundred years? Listen to the new lines of thought that have arisen in that time. Intelligence has been flowering among all races and the need for self-expression and self-pride can no longer be denied to anyone. Women are demanding that they be recognized as thinking and intelligent beings, which they are, of course. This has been a shock to older men, who see the invasion of women into the work place as improper. To them, a woman should be at home, taking care of the children (and, of course, all the needs of the man). That thinking should never have been. Of course, a woman brings children into the world and takes care of them, teaches them and raises them to adulthood, but this is also meant to be a part of the man's responsibility. The woman's mind, during this time, does not go into a coma, or it should not. A woman is a soul entity who has been both man and woman many times since its creation, and all of the lessons and experiences are as much in a woman's subconscious as in a man's. There is essentially no difference in the thinking processes between man and woman. The difference lies in the physical makeup that distinguishes the sexes in matter. The woman expresses the soft and sensitive part of nature and the man expresses the strength and the dynamic energies of nature. These two parts are meant to work together to form a whole, and they always have. A woman is not going against nature when she uses her mind to create and earn a living, but she finds it difficult when she tries to mold her nature into that of a man. That is where the mixup begins.

In the inner being of a woman there is the memory of the male nature; in the inner being of a man there is the memory of the female nature. It is a balance of what every soul entity really is and this is what keeps each person on solid ground. A man would be a savage beast if he did not feel the female traits of compassion and love; a woman would dissolve into a pool of emotion if she did not have the reserves of strength and determination that her male traits represent. As in all things, without that balance, humanity could not exist.

In a relationship there must be a balance also. Partners must contribute the feelings and traits that are their inheritance from the Creator. By combining the best of both, there is a bond created, a cohesive unit that cannot easily be broken. When one partner tries to overwhelm the other with his or her abilities or feelings, the balance is broken and the second partner is left feeling unworthy at best and a bond slave at worst. Then the cohesive whole breaks apart and the unit must dissolve.

It is time for all individuals to look into themselves and find the real person within, to understand the role he or she needs to play in this lifetime. One should not have to bear all the burdens of a relationship; it must be a shared lifetime, with the energy flows of each individual open to the other in trust, harmony and love.

I hear this question all the time: "What does God think of us, living together without being married? Will we be forgiven?" The "Bonds of Matrimony" were given to mankind in order to create a family unit to give children born of a physical union the love, security and teaching that a human child needs in order to have a solid foundation in life. The pattern is there to be used. When it is not used and a child is involved, the damage it does to the child is rapidly apparent. Mankind was given, and still has, the gift of free will. There is no tribunal waiting in the wings to severely punish those who do not follow the Ten Commandments. The damage you do to yourself by not following them will follow you into the next dimension upon your bodily death and there you must deal with it yourself.

It is understandable to us that many young people fear marriage and commitment because of the high divorce rates they see around them. Single parents struggle to bring up their children and exist on a small salary. There is never a guarantee that a relationship will succeed, but the effort to make it succeed seems to be lacking in many marriages. When one partner sees marriage as a setup where he or she will be taken care of by the other and life will be one long love affair, it is not surprising that it fails when the realities of life come into focus.

People of all ages today have the availability of good counseling, many books on the subject of relationships and simply their own ears and good judgment to rely upon. Sex is no longer a romantic mystery; it is flouted constantly on the radio, TV and media publications of all sorts. It has become a game or just something to do on a date. Sometimes men and women marry just to assure themselves of a permanent sex partner. What a sorry and shallow idea. With all of this confusion around, it becomes a very difficult decision for a person to make — a lifelong search to find the right person who can fulfill the inner spiritual needs as well as the physical needs and the need for companionship that goes so much deeper than just a casual liaison. How do you make that decision? Where do you find such a person?

It is universal law that one cannot love another until he or she learns to love himself or herself first. A soul entity living on your planet must peel away the layers of social teachings, fear, mistrust, self-degradation, self-consciousness, hatreds and so forth until it arrives at its real inner being, the soul or person it really is. It must find the beauty of itself, realize the good things it has done during this lifetime and be happy with the being it is. When it encounters events that it is not happy with or is ashamed of, the time has come for forgiveness. God grants forgiveness instantly; people forgive themselves very infrequently. Without forgiving yourself, the pain goes on indefinitely, and the being within cannot come forth because the outer being does not feel it is worthy to accept it. Forgive and rid yourself of such feelings; the hurt and guilt will fall like leaves from your shoulders and you will feel clean and refreshed.

At this point, fall in love with yourself again. Rejoice in the being you are and the fact that you have been given the priceless privilege of living a lifetime on this beautiful planet. Realize that you are only half of a whole until you become joined with your opposite polarity. When you are clear within yourself and the vibrations go forth in clarity to others, one who sees that your vibrations reflect his or her own will eventually come to you. Like attracts like, don't forget. If you wish to attract a loving, sensitive and responsible person, you must become a loving, sensitive and responsible person to start with. When two people with clear, loving vibrations come together, there will be no problems as to whether or not that person will leave you, betray you or treat you badly. The union has been made and the happiness created by it will last forever. The problem in finding permanent relationships in your time is not in finding the right person; it is that the seekers are not sending out the right signals because they are too confused about what and who they want, where they really are and where they want to be. First things first.

The seeking and finding of the spiritual being that is you is not only for the purpose of finding a mate or companion, but is essential in order to live a lifetime of contentment and creativity and to enable you to accomplish the goal that you came into this life to attain. Wandering around in confusion results in depression, guilt and feelings of unworthiness. No soul entity is unworthy of being, or it would not have arrived in matter. Work to shed these faulty layers of false feelings; listen to the guidance from within instead of commercial lies being fed to you constantly. Learn to discern the foolish repetitions trying to entrap you into believing you must have this or that, or look this way or that, or think what they want you to think. Think for yourselves; see for yourselves; recognize the underlying greed behind the mind-bending going on. Find for yourselves what you really need or want; it is specific only for you. How you look should be as you see yourselves, not as you think others want you to look. Inventory all of the "things" you own; do they really please you? Do you really need or use them? Or did you buy them because it was the "thing" to do, the current fad you must have? Life is too precious to spend it wastefully in the senseless seeking after "things" or the pleasures or "highs" that leave you empty inside, especially when these things are not really pleasing to you. Look within to see what really does please you. Perhaps a beautiful picture or design makes you feel good when you look at it; that would be a good thing to acquire. Would you really enjoy taking a walk in a forest instead of going to a crowded and smoky bar? With a little effort, that can be accomplished. Don't be coerced into doing things the real you does not enjoy doing. Be what you truly are. Do you think everyone will make fun of you? If they do, they are being false to themselves. Far more of your contemporaries will respect you for being true to yourselves and envy you for being able to do so. If you must live with a partner without a commitment, so be it. It is up to you. Perhaps there is a deep feeling between you and you don't really want to give up the relationship, yet there are factors, known or known, that make you afraid to make the commitment. Perhaps the unknown factor lies within. To be really brave, I suggest that both of you do some serious digging into yourselves. Then, when you have a better grasp on who you are, get to know each other all over again to see if the relationship is right. If you need help, there are many very good commercial and spiritual counselors who could give you some good insights along the way. "True love" is real. But it only exists when each partner is true to him- or herself as well as to his or her loved one.

Before you take steps that will create an unwanted or unloved child, think back to your own childhood. If you were raised in a loving and secure atmosphere, think how it would have been if you had not had that loving family. If you grew up in conditions of hate, loneliness or desertion, do you want that for your children? For a man and a woman, creating a new human being is a tremendous responsibility, one that will follow the parent all his or her life and all subsequent lifetimes. If that responsibility is shrugged off and the child is deprived of its needs by that parent, the resulting karma will follow the parent until he or she has to go through the same agony. This is universal law, not to be disregarded. If a child is created from a rape situation, the rapist has put upon himself a heavy load which will increase until he pays the price for it. Civil law may extract its penalty, but spiritual law is even harsher. Beware. The child created from a rape comes into the lifetime with the knowledge that it will not have a loving family and must strive very hard to make it a worthwhile lifetime. This will be perhaps the soul of one who created a child in the past in that manner.

It cannot be expected that all marriages will be a perfect union of spirit and matter. There are very many who, without knowing these things I have just mentioned, instinctively know that the right person has appeared, and their union is a happy, lifelong waltz through life. Those who are trying very hard to find the right partner sometimes mistakenly think they have found the love of their life, stay together for perhaps a long time, but then when they become more aware of their inner beings, they find that the relationship has become unbalanced; the other person has become a stranger, and the union breaks apart. That is not entirely a bad thing, because then each of the partners can be free to search for one who will be part of a blending that can be a perfect mixture for all time.

During any relationship, remember that you are a full one-half of that blending; but, because you are fully a spiritual being, your effort must be 100%; your love must be given 100%; your understanding of the other must be 100%. Anything held back from your loved one will be felt strongly and resented. When you give yourself to your loved one in a fully committed relationship, nothing must be withheld. "Becoming one" means just that. It is a blending, an understanding, a total giving. Anything less than that is a forgery. No one can give his or her all and exist closely with another who gives only a small percentage of him- or herself. If the opening to another cannot be done, leave quietly and find the one to whom you can give this gift.

If an unhappy marriage exists, do not think that you can fool the child or children into thinking everything is all right. Children are most sensitive to emotions and the deception is really more hurtful to them than being told the truth. If a separation must be made, please make the truth very clear to the children: that you and your partner are unhappy together and must live apart, that the children did nothing to force the issue and were not a reason for the separation. Give them all of your love and make arrangements for them to live with the person who can care for them the best, but be sure they know the other parent loves them very much and will be with them as much as possible. Mean that, and do it! The children of broken marriages are becoming a separate group in your society and at least have each other to go to for understanding and compassion.

I hope to give encouragement in this lesson, although it sounds rather "down" in content. This is because we have great sadness for the broken homes and broken hearts that abound in the world. So many changes are coming into being now that it is not surprising that so much confusion exists. Higher frequencies of vibrations enfolding the Earth now are putting inner pressures on all of you and not making things easier. It is a hard time and it will get worse as the end of this age draws near. Please make prayer a part of your lives; be aware of the inner guidance that is being sent more strongly each day; know that there are spiritual friends who are trying to help you in every way we can. Just call on us! If you do become aware of your inner being, this time can be the most thrilling and enriching lifetime that any soul entity has ever had; the possibilities are unlimited!

It all starts within, where the real you and the Christ Spirit reside. That is a union above all others that will make your lifetime in matter a heaven on Earth indeed, when that relationship is understood.

God Bless You All.

The Golden Path

CHAPTER TWENTY-ONE

Rest in the Lord

By Master Teacher Hilarian
1991

T he season of Fall changes the life forces in the world so that growing things have a chance to rest and renew themselves once more. The cycles that the Lord created are beautiful indeed.

So does the cycle of life emerge from the depth of one's being when the Earth signals changes in vibrations. Human bodies respond to these cycles also in that there is a feeling of an approaching time to rest from the labors of the fields during the cold months, renewing energies for spring plantings.

Alas, civilization has plotted against this natural way of things and demands that mankind work hard all of the seasons of the year, giving only a week, two weeks or (rarely) a month to rest. When humanity does have that time of rest, the time is usually spent in hurrying up to travel somewhere to exhaust themselves in trying to play or visit different places, so that returning to the workplace is a relief!

Mankind seems to feel guilty about resting. In primitive times, they had to work all the time just to keep themselves fed and protected. Now, such is not the case, but the instinct to keep on the go constantly still prevails. And this is the cause of many of humanity's ills. The Creator decreed in the beginning that man should rest one day out of the seven. This was given because the human body needs this rest, and real rest is what was and is meant. Rest for the body and rest for the mind.

How few people really know how to rest! Watching television is not resting, because it stimulates the mind. Reading is not resting, because the body has to hold the book and the mind is busy assimilating what is on the printed page. Sitting and talking is not resting, because one is listening to another and creating his or her own part of the conversation, which may or may not be a pleasant one. Lying still and thinking of all that is going on in life, perhaps planning the next thing to do or worrying about what is present in the life is not resting, because it puts stress on the nerves which are tensing to get up and do something.

Rest means that the body should be completely relaxed in a quiet atmosphere, if possible. The nervous system should be at rest, relaxed and quiet. The mind should still its busy murmurings and be soothed by the sounds of nature or, perhaps, some quiet, beautiful music. It should be a time for the body and mind to heal themselves of the stresses and difficulties encountered during the day and to energize themselves to start again in a better frame of mind. No, this is not sleep I am describing; it is simply resting.

Mankind must learn to take better care of the mind and body. In the past 100 years the trend toward constant work and thought has damaged mankind and brought on ills that insidiously wear down the body's defenses because of the lack of energy.

Please make the time during each day, even for an hour if need be, to really rest. Learn to turn off the busy mind and simply lie down and be quiet. You will know when your body is ready to get going again. Yes, it will take some practice, for the first instinct is to remember something and jump up again after five minutes. If you persevere, however, you will rise with a feeling of lightness and renewal; the mind will be clearer and the problems of the day will become easier to solve. After a few weeks, you will find your body becoming more energetic and little colds or viruses will not attach themselves to you as often.

There are stressful times coming in the years to come. You need to bring your bodies and minds to their best condition. Strength and clarity are always given from the Lord when you ask. Remember that they are there, within, and they can be reached when you allow yourself to find them in the peaceful content of rest.

The phrase "Rest in the Lord" reveals its meaning now. It means to allow the mind and body to relax in peaceful rest so that the Divine Being who dwells within can be at one with you.

Yes, rest in the Lord.

Blessings upon you now and always.

CHAPTER TWENTY-TWO

Angels

By Master Teacher Peter
1990

Master Peter: We are receiving many different teachings regarding angels. Please explain what angels are; how and when they were created (are they continuously created?); if they have anything to do with entities leaving lifetimes on this plane; their duties? Do they communicate with those serving incarnations on this plane? If so, to what purpose? Do they have form? Why have they appeared to us as winged beings? How many "guardian" angels are assigned to each incarnated entity? How do they integrate their work with the entity's higher self?

The Angelic Cordon is a created mass of entities formed for a singular purpose: to be servants of the Most High Creator. They were created long before the Christ was formed as a Cocreator with the Almighty and before the Thought of God brought forth the soul entities who now crowd universes of time and space. As I understand it, no new angels have been created since the first creation of the angelic forces of God.

When soul entities were formed out of the mass of intelligence and energy that is God, the term you are familiar with, angels, were summoned to work with each new soul entity to guide, guard and teach, in limited circumstances. They are essentially guardians and guides who help each soul entity find its way through the centuries. The number of angels assigned to each soul entity varies depending upon the velocity of its trip through eternity, the wisdom it has accumulated, the help needed for a specific project the soul entity has set up for itself before incarnating and many other factors. A highly developed soul entering your plane for the purpose of being a teacher may have only one attending angel to smooth out the rough spots when asked. Others who, comparatively speaking, are just starting on their paths will have as many as ten or eleven angels helping them along. The number of angels will vary during the lifetime, also. When the specific need for an angel has passed, it will be sent to other assignments.

Angels are multifaceted. At their creation, they were given infinite knowledge which, in turn, gives them the ability to help in whatever situation they are needed. Scientists, artists, creators of all kinds find their ideas and sparks of creativity flowing from their attending angels. As you understand it, angels must be asked before help is given. This is true in most cases. However, when an angel is attending an entity who is placed in your third dimension to accomplish certain things, thoughts and ideas may be given as a method of getting the entity started (a jump-start, so to speak).

All communications from the world of spirit, including the angelic forces, are filtered through the higher soulself of each entity. Much used to be said about "controls" for mediums. Fancy names were sometimes given for such controls, but they were all the higher selves of the mediums. Each higher self is the prime protector for the entity. All help, guidance or communication from the angels or other higher-dimensional beings must pass the threshold of the guardian higher soulself. Even if the help or information is very well-intentioned by the giver, if the higher self knows it not to be right for the entity, it will be intercepted and turned away.

Requests from a soul entity for help and guidance from the Almighty One are sent through the higher self without hindrance, as commanded by God. Each and every prayer or communication to the Creator is heard, noted and taken care of in the best way for the entity. No prayer is ever unheeded or ignored. Humanity still has to learn that the thoughts of the Most High are the only thoughts that are able to see clearly what is best for each individual. "Father knows best" has a familiar ring to it!

Angels do sometimes communicate directly with an incarnated entity, if the entity calls upon them for a specific reason. They will then declare themselves to be an angel(s) and give the entity a name or names to call them by. This is for the entity's convenience, since all interdimensional beings are known by their vibrations, not by Earthly names.

There are angels who have risen very high in the presence of the Most High. You know them as archangels. They have the responsibility of assigning the mass of guardian angels their duties and observing whether they are needed or not. Do they hold the keys to Heaven? What a charming idea. They do, perhaps, but only in the sense of, again, assigning those who are to help those entities returning into spirit. Many highly spiritual entities returning from a lifetime on Earth will request assignment to help their fellow beings coming back; these requests are handled by the archangels and assignments made. They are monitored and, when the need of such service is over, the soul is given the choices of additional learning, teaching, traveling, and so on, as it pleases. The soul still has and always will have the choice of free will. That is a commandment of the Most High that will never change. Only angels are under the direct control of the archangels and the Most High; their will is to do the Creator's Will.

No human being will ever have a better friend and confidant than his or her angels. Even in little things, they are always there to help you in distress, pain, unhappiness or indecision. No request for assistance is ever turned away. There is never a time when your angels are busy at something else and do not hear you; their whole concern is you and are always "on tap." Their line is never busy.

Remember, however, that this angelic helper situation is merely that, just helpers. Any real need for help or decisions must and shall always be directed first to the Most High. Angels are given their duties from the decisions and directions of the Creator. Angels cannot make decisions on their own. They were sent as messengers many times, some of them recorded in your Bible. Note: as messengers only! They relayed information as they were told; they made no decisions on their own. They can be addressed regarding little things, but address the important issues to the Creator alone.

Winged beings? Spirits don't need wings. They go where their thoughts send them. Humans long ago could not conceive of transportation without some kind of assistance, so a being they felt flew in the air would certainly need wings; a natural summation in those times. Today, there are still many people who associate angels with wings and the angels cheerfully comply with this, even though amused by it, if this makes the entity feel better. Sometimes angels will announce themselves by shadows of wings upon a wall or by a flapping sound, as of wings. It all depends on the personality involved. More often, when an angel wishes to establish a conscious communication with its assigned entity, there will be a feeling of warmth, love and perhaps a slight rosy glow in the entity's vicinity. There are so many variations, I cannot begin to list them. Each angel has its own way of communicating and helping its entity.

When you feel you need a cool breeze, a parking spot, a little consideration from some situation, ask your angel. They make your life a lot more pleasant and less lonely.

Bless you and bless your angels.

CHAPTER TWENTY-THREE

Energizing
Your Life

By Master Teacher Kathumi
1993

As you walk down a city street or a country road, there are usually thoughts of everyday life milling around in your mind. In the city, probably financial matters, the day of work ahead or what to have for dinner. Even in the country, one's personal problems seem to shut out everything else. May I make a suggestion? Even in the city, nature abounds all about you. Even if the sky far above the skyscrapers is all that is visible, you can still feel enfolded in the energies that created the planet, all things in nature and you.

You may think of energy as something created by hydroelectric or atomic plants. That is artificial energy. What I am speaking of is the creative universal energy that is part of every living thing, that moves constantly, creating the new and transforming the dying or worn-out to new creative life. The life force that provides you with the energy to move, speak and live your daily lives is moving into your cells constantly. If it did not, you would be a form made of inert matter, housing a spiritual being that would have no way to express itself.

All life in your dimension is a form of energy that ebbs and flows, just as your oceans, in some respects very fast, in others, very slowly. You can feel this life force in others, even if you are not aware of it in yourselves. You can feel the dynamic force flowing out of a high-powered executive or highly-motivated creative artist. It fills a room when such a person walks in. You can feel the very low ebb of energy in a person who is morose or dejected.

Now, feel it in yourselves. Take several very deep breaths and hold them for a few seconds before releasing them out of the body. You will find it very relaxing. That is energy restoring your cells and nerves. Now, do this again perhaps ten times in a row. You will feel light-headed for a few minutes as the brain adjusts itself to the increased energy flow. Recognize this for what it is. Those who meditate use this practice to clear their minds of sluggish thoughts or feelings in order to present a clear path to their inner selves. In everyday life, do not make fun of the "health nut" who stands in front of his or her window in the morning breathing in great gulps of fresh air. Isn't that person the one who accomplishes a great deal throughout the day? This brings new oxygen and energy to the cells and energizes the body. Are oxygen and universal energy the same thing? No. Oxygen is part of the elements that make up your atmosphere; universal energy is the life force that animates all things. Breathing deeply in the mornings and stretching the body is an excellent way to wake up the mind and body for the day's activities. The fresher the air, the better, but better stuffy, heated air than nothing. Even in that situation, energy is there.

Is energy intake something that can be controlled? Absolutely. Your mind is ever in control of your body and the energy that you allow to flow into it. If you block it out by disturbing or depressing thoughts, the flow of energy is cut off. Did you ever see a person in that frame of mind who was full of creative energy? You have heard of persons who have decided to die, and have simply lain down and died. It is possible, though a terrible waste. They simply blocked out all life-giving energy as well as refused to let the body be nourished by the food they ate. Oh yes, the mind is that powerful. But by opening your mind to thoughts full of possibility, learning, creativity and the love of life itself, this universal energy of life flows freely and abundantly into your structure to nourish all the cells that operate your mind and body. Even if problems beset you, deal with them as quickly as you can and open your mind to new inflows of this energy. If and when you do, problems become more understandable, solutions appear as if by magic, and life is easier to cope with. You have often been told that it is better not to make decisions when tired or angry, that "sleeping on it" makes it easier to see things in a different light in the morning. These are all ways of resting the mind and allowing universal creative energy to flow unrestricted once more.

In nature, there are no such blockages, except when mankind pollutes the air around vegetation so that energy cannot flow uninterruptedly. Even though the soil is still feeding the plant, it turns brown and lifeless when natural energy cannot reach the cells in the plant itself. Chemicals in the soil that are thought to nourish plant life thicken root systems until energy in the soil is prevented from entering the plant. Reliance upon chemicals simply substitutes the best and natural energy flow for an artificial one that eventually distorts the cells and seeds of the plant world. When withdrawn, the plant can no longer function normally. It is the same with a person whose energy is restricted, as if the person were enveloped in a large plastic bag filled with a substitute gas for air and forced to live in it all his or her life. The seed passed down to his or her children would have the same propensity for unnatural gas and would not be able to live in the free, clean air of Earth. How foolish this all is. If you farm or garden, please take this to heart. Mother Earth renews her soil constantly with great amounts of natural energy that flows constantly through and around the planet. If left for a short time to renew itself, a worn-out field will become ready to plant again. Old farmers knew this very well, but greed has forced mankind into planting on land that is tired and feeding it with fertilizers to pep it up so that crops will grow all year round.

What does this do to food grown on such land? It is not really harmful, as the fertilizers are quite diluted by the time that produce reaches your table, but the natural energy that should have been present in the food is simply not there. You might as well be eating cardboard, seasoned and flavored to taste.

Creatures of the air flourish all the time, unless the air has become contaminated. Their cheerful songs in the morning are a herald to all that life is beautiful and that energy is yours for the accepting. They are constantly on the go, rarely resting until nightfall. They freely accept the natural flow of energy as they were given the instinct to do by their Creator. Follow their lead.

Heavy clothing does not stop the energy inflow, but heavy artificial fabrics can do so to some extent, if you are covered by them for the most part. Energy will penetrate and flow through all natural fabrics, even leather. Plastics have a very concentrated cellular structure that presents a barrier to energy flow. Try to wear them in moderation and not over the entire body. It is well to have as much of the body open to air as possible. Plastic rainwear keeps moisture away from the body, but it also prevents the wonderfully fresh moisture-enriched air from reaching you. Moisture in air increases energy in the cells of creation and condenses the strength of energy. When you go out after a downpour, it is almost exciting to breathe the fresh moisture-rich air; it makes one feel more alive. Remember that. It does. A walk in the rain under an umbrella gives one a rich inflow of energy that cannot be mistaken. Don't teach your children to rush inside at the first sprinkle. If it is warm, let them feel the delicious taste of rain upon their tongues and receive moisture into their skin; it is good for them. Even if mud is an awful mess to clean up, think of the combination of energy-rich rain and energy-rich soil combining into a delightful creation to play in. All children have a natural urge to play in mud for this reason. And if it is raining at the same time, all the better! Now you mothers are upset with me. Even so, try to recognize the benefits your children will receive. How alive they are when returning from such play! Even better, join them!

Recognize that there is restorative energy flowing all around you at all times. Keep your thoughts, attitudes and emotions open and life will be beautifully healthy and creatively satisfying.

Have a wonderful day!

CHAPTER TWENTY-FOUR

Life in the Universe

By Master Teacher Peter
1990

Since the dawn of time in the world of matter there have been spiritual beings who dwell within that world of matter. They are servants of the Most High, sent to control the stirrings of movement upon the planet. Ocean currents, air and wind currents, even the inner movements of the planet are under strict control by the Almighty through these spirits. You have heard various teachings regarding beings who live within Earth. These are Earth spirits. They have no form as you know it; indeed they could not have because of the heat and pressures that exist near the core. They move through the interior of your globe, balancing and releasing pressures that build up in the planet by way of energy releases from many vortexes around the globe, volcanic eruptions, earthquakes and positive and negative energies being received and released at your North and South Poles. They do not concern themselves with humans and animals that live on the surface so that their judgments concerning what they do will not be affected.

Eastern religions recognize these spirits as devas, but they have been called many other names down through the centuries. Under the devas, and under their control, there are many less powerful spirits who work in all strata of nature. The "little people" of the Irish, the fairies of all countries fall into this category. Large forests are full of these "little spirits" because of the myriad species of growing things and wildlife.

When you go into a forest, sit down quietly; relax and feel the earth beneath you; take into your senses the vibrations of all that is around you; become a part of it. You might not see anything out of the ordinary, but you will feel the presence of millions of life forms swirling through the space where you are sitting.

Mankind is almost totally unaware of the vibrant life energy that makes up the world. Things are seen, yes, but mostly they are unseen. In your third dimension, there are subdimensions that contain the unseen spirit workers. It is not unlike your subconscious being, which controls your bodily functions without your conscious awareness. So it is that nature also has a subdimension in which the workings of nature are directed. All patterns in the universe are repeated at many levels.

Yes, there is a degree of consciousness in all things. There has to be or nature could not respond to the directions of the Creator. Even the very grains of sand that adhere to each other to form a rock follow the universal direction to do so. How could the cells of your body work together so perfectly and in balance with the body as a whole if they were not able to receive the directions from the subconscious to do their job? All things in the universe are under the direction of the Almighty One, from the creation of galaxies to the placement of an atom. Is it then so hard to believe that there are millions of His "employees" working behind the scenes to accomplish His great works? And that these workers start at very high-dimensional spiritual levels and progress down to very small spiritual beings that direct the bloom of the flowers?

The universe is a highly complex organization of life. Its "directors" are those who have been created to oversee all that is. They have been termed by humanity the Hierarchy. Each member of the Hierarchy has its own sphere of management and is under the close direction of the Creator. I use the word "it" because they are beings of intense Light and do not have male or female characteristics. Unfortunately, in your language, there are no words that express a highly intelligent "it." Those who realize that the Creator also is not a "He" often use the word "It" to describe the unimaginable intelligence and power that is God. Even though that word in your language is entirely insufficient to express that Being of Light, mankind must simply come to understand the real meaning.

Let us go back to the devas. Again, there is no English word to describe them, so "devas" it will be.

The devas are only a little lower than the angels in the spiritual family. They have great power and reign supreme over the areas to which they are sent to rule. Each organized country has its own deva; every large area of open or mountainous country has a deva. Each ocean has a deva. They direct the forces of nature for their area but do not interfere in the lives of mankind.

The human family was created directly from the essence of God, and retains a portion of the power, creative force and knowledge of the Creator. Therefore, there is a direct line of communication between the embodied soul spirit and the Creator. That inner communication is the direction that people receive, and incarnated soul entities are directed by no other being or power.

The dark forces, consisting of those who were cast out of the presence of God ages ago, were empowered by the Creator to reside in your world to give each soul entity a negative force against which to balance the positive force of the Creator. It is this dance between the positive and negative which makes up the world of matter. It would not be possible without it.

Negative forces in your lives give you the incentive to pull toward the positive actions and thoughts. They are the "down side" which humanity has the choice to accept or reject. Even in the darkness of the night hours, there is beauty and peace; so it is within the dark forces. Behind the evil faces that are presented, realize they are beings created by the Father of All. The dark forces are undergoing a learning process also and most of these dark angels will return to the Father eventually. When the world has gone through its cleansing, those who still cannot accept the Light of Truth will be sent to another universe to continue their lessons. Remember, nothing created by the Father of All is ever destroyed, except by its own determined desire. If a soul comes to a point where it simply does not wish to continue, it has the consent of God, by free will, to simply snuff itself out. This is a very rare thing in the universe, since the sense of life is very strong and the love of God is a beautiful thing to experience and live within.

Be aware of all creation; know that there is life and love all around you, no matter where you are or what you are feeling. Open your senses to the energies that are moving around you. Feel the love and communication that is always going on. There is no such thing as what you call a "hunch." It is a piece of communication that has pierced your mind for your benefit. Be thankful when you receive them.

What you term teachers and guides are your guardian angels and those fourth-, fifth- and sixth-dimensional beings who have been assigned to help guide you through your lifetime on Planet Earth. They speak to you through your inner self and, when you are ready, through your mind. Some soul entities are able to hear their voices. They are there helping in many little ways that some of you do not even recognize and call "coincidences." A coincidence is a rare occurrence. Without the interference of their spiritual helpers, people would find themselves in trouble constantly. The small changes made all the time to prevent their charges from stubbing their toes, so to speak, keep the spiritual helpers very busy.

When you begin to acknowledge all of this life around, inside and above your physical being, you will begin to really become a part of the splendid creation that the Father has placed on your planet. Sensing the love and the life will make you more alive and the realization of that life will enhance your purpose for being here.

Given in love

CHAPTER TWENTY-FIVE

The Peace of God

By the Beings of Light
1992

Whenever there are situations in life that are stressful, upsetting and downright frightening, it is rare that the thought of just being alone somewhere and feeling peaceful does not come. Peace is the most desired feeling in the world, but what is it? The angels announced at the birth of Jesus that He came to bring peace, but where has it disappeared to?

Was peace always present on the Earth, or did Jesus bring it with Him? Is peace something real and valid, or is it a lack of negative actions? How does one find peace when a real understanding of it seems too slippery to hold on to?

For centuries the terms "war" and "peace" have continued to stir up turmoil in the world. War is well understood; destruction of material things and the killing of humans as well as every other living thing in the way of a military advance has almost become the norm. Hollywood makes millions of dollars every year by reenacting the most violent interactions between human beings they can think of. The effect of this constant diet of negativity is producing a race of young people whose hearts are cold and unfeeling toward others. All that seems to be important is to be the "winner." All violence or negative actions against even a single embodied entity is war.

The innocents (and we define those people as not having a say in the reasons for a war or the factors controlled by the commanding officers) are always in the middle. Since World War II, the ancient ways of war that decreed that soldiers must only fight soldiers on the proper battlefields have faded into the past. Wars are now waged on city streets, in public buildings and even private homes. Death has become a minor issue, just a way of clearing the way for the conquerors. In many countries, young men are raised to believe that they kill for the sake of Allah, Christ or whoever the rulers choose to bear the blame. When they are recruited for service, there is no hesitation to kill anyone, even children and babies. The natural protective instinct for the preservation of the species has been erased from their minds. That is war today, still prevailing in parts of Europe, Africa and other small countries that get little publicity.

When a cessation of the fighting finally comes to pass, it is called peace. Most times, peace is an extremely fragile thing, easily broken if someone makes the wrong move or says the wrong thing. When a complete end to warfare is accomplished, it takes many years of reconstruction, many hours of counseling for returning soldiers and civilian survivors in order to at least calm the fears and the nightmares to a point where they can cope with life again. There is very little peace in all that anguish. Years later, things are back to normal, factories are manufacturing new materials and inventions for peacetime use that originated on the battlefields and people are leading lives of reasonable prosperity. This is peace in a way; it is a lack of fearing attack and want.

Today your great nation and the so-called super powers are not actively engaged in warfare and are at peace. Are they? The undertow of competition, races for corporate leadership, tension, pressures, all are taken for granted. Is living in a lovely home with all the comforts money can buy construed to be a peaceful existence?

There is only one source of peace — the Eternal Blessed Creator of the universe. There is only one way to obtain the real thing for oneself: creating a real relationship with the spiritual being that you are. This is accomplished through a determined decision on your part that this is your goal. The constantly racing mind must be slowed and halted for a time; then the flow of conscious yearning and honest desire to become one with God is started toward that inner being that goes by many names today: the higher self, the cosmic self, the higher consciousness and so forth. It is all one real higher intelligence that is part of you and that tries to guide you through your Earthly existence. This higher self is part of the upper dimensions of reality and is fully connected to them.

The concept of "All Are One" is hard for some people to accept because they have become used to trying all their lives to be better than someone else and have more than the people next door, to be racially aloof from those they consider below their social status. It is said that when all people walk around in the nude, status vanishes. Imagine how it will be when the vibrations of all mankind are raised simultaneously to a dimension where all beings are recognized by vibrations alone! Bodies will no longer be solid and will require less or nothing made of matter to sustain them. There will be an instant knowing that each created soul or entity is the beloved child of the Most High, that no one is higher in the love of God than another. Can't you imagine the utter outrage of the powerful leaders of the world to find themselves in such a position? Can you picture the wonderful sense of belonging of those who have wandered the world alone and in want? We are told that soul entities who refuse to give up their greed and power to enter into the total oneness of love will find themselves on a different world or plane, there to start their education all over again. God does not hurt or punish His children; they are simply lovingly given the chance to learn over again, and again, until the fierce negative strains that rule their thoughts are put away forever.

Peace is the total lack of strain, pressure, tension of any kind, a sensation of total relaxation over the entire body, a mind at rest, free from guilt, fear and driving ambitions. It is a feeling of perfect contentment and rest, safe in the Father's Arms. There is a sense of closeness with God and all living things.

Most people find the center for this peace in the heart area of their bodies. This is the central place of energy in the body, called the heart chakra. This is the place where the love of God abides. Love and peace cannot be separated, for where one dwells, the other will always reside.

Peace and love are choices, not gifts to be given indiscriminately. The path of life is a difficult one indeed and one of many different choices. The most important thing to be taught is that peace and love are there, within you, waiting for each person to recognize. Even with a minute opening of the mind to that knowledge, a crack is created that leaks out tantalizing moments of that peace and love so that the seeker will be able to define what it is that is being sought. It is a goal highest above all others, for peace is your connection with God.

For most, it takes many years to travel the short distance into that blessed part of your body. All of the trials and tribulations of Earthly life seem determined to pull you apart and keep your mind in constant strife with the realities of worldly life. It takes courage, planning for quiet time, no matter what, and the constant seeking of that inner haven. The Father of All places no restraints or difficulties in your way; it is your own mind and Earthly ambitions that create the walls and hurdles. It is your own determination, with the help of your spiritual counselors when you ask them, that will bring you at last to that beautiful place.

Peace is the connection with the higher dimensions of spirit that you will come home to when it is time to leave the body behind. It is a taste of the eternal oneness and love that is the spiritual kingdom.

The times spent in that peace and love within are to be cherished and returned to whenever possible. Having the knowingness within your conscious mind that you can find the peace when you need it creates a valuable cushion for all of the downfalls of life. There is no longer the feeling of utter hopelessness or helplessness. You know that hope and help are always available to you. When others are hateful and selfish, mean and unforgiving, you are able to feel sympathy for their condition. Understanding of all mankind increases each time you reach out to others to find that part of God within them. Forgiveness then becomes perfectly natural; it is an aspect of God.

Finding the inner place of peace will often erase the hard lessons you have come to learn, because the answers to problems will come clearly and instantly. You will then be free to work hand-in-hand with your Creator to help others find the same freedom.

Seek within and you will find. Bring that love to the surface and share it with all you meet; it will reflect back to you. When mankind comes of age with this full realization, then, truly, there will be peace on Earth!

We send you our understanding, love and guidance. All you need to do is accept it.

CHAPTER TWENTY-SIX

The Light for Humanity

By Master Teacher Sananda
1991

Worldwide, the message is being sent today that the Prince of Peace is overshadowing each embodied spiritual being on your planet. This presence is becoming stronger every year, approaching the time when His rule will be fully recognized in the time of new beginnings. The Christ Spirit has always been part of the higher consciousness of every spiritual being, but only in the past 100 years has this fact begun to be recognized on a conscious level by most human beings.

The Christ is now increasing His presence and making it so strong that mankind will find it hard to dismiss the inner feelings of peace and the need to find the truth. The presence is expressing itself as an inner pressure to those who have denied it for so long, to the point of being decidedly uncomfortable to live with. It is arising as a need for action, for love, for recognition of self, a need to be outdoors where nature is alive and vibrant, a need to be with other people and share the feelings that are so strong and undeniable.

As those who have opened their hearts already to the Christ within feel this presence even more strongly, the need to share this expanding inner Light becomes foremost in the consciousness. Groups of Light Workers everywhere are increasing and people are pulled to them as a moth to the flame. When home groups become too crowded, there will be those who will be inspired to start new groups and opportunities for sharing and teaching. There are so many who need to know and need to be taught the basic truths they have never heard. Let your Lights shine!

Churches all over the world are coming to life again. Governments who have denied even the entrance to churches are now allowing their people to come together to worship again in the beautiful cathedrals and churches that have been vacant for so long. In China, although the populace is denied religion by the government, people are coming together in secret, pushed and pulled by the longing and the pressure of spirit to worship the Creator of All and to study the Word of God. It is not only the old people who have memories of a church life who are flocking to the altars of the world, but especially younger people who are finding this need irresistible. Remember, most of the young people of today are those very old and knowledgeable souls who have entered your world to teach and help humanity cope with the changes to come. They are very close to the Father and their higher consciousnesses. Even if born into a communistic belief situation, it is not long before the inner guidance tells them there is more, much more.

The media go into long detail about the ills and woes of the world, but they are missing what is really happening. The higher consciousness of humanity is knocking, and humanity is opening the doors in ever-increasing numbers. "New Age" books are being channeled and written in abundance and from every point of view possible so that all mankind will be able to understand what is being given, no matter what the background of the reader.

It may seem that there is so much on the market already that it is useless to try to write more. It is not useless! It is imperative that the writing be continued as strongly as possible.

As time draws nearer to the coming of the New Age, many new pronouncements will be made by the Father of All and transmitted to channels who are receiving knowledge from the higher dimensions. This news must be given to the world as soon as possible. The Holy Ones are commissioned by the Father to transmit this knowledge and they are doing so all over the world. The United States has no jurisdiction on this. The truth is being transmitted in many ways, according to the ability of each part of the world to listen and to learn.

It would be ideal if such written information could be distributed free of charge to everyone who wished to have it, but, unfortunately, the world runs in a way that forces channels and writers to carry the expenses of such endeavors. It is human nature, in this world of commerce, to feel that the higher the price paid for an object, the more valuable it is. If something is given too freely, it is deemed of no worth. Look at yourselves carefully in this respect, for whatever you are able to receive, whether at great cost or at nominal cost, must be studied carefully as to the contents. If what you are reading is truth, you will know it. If it is not, there will be a feeling of negativity, of the desire to put the material away and not read it. *Truth is like a magnet; it will draw you to it.* When you go to a book store, are you not drawn to certain books or written material? Are you not repelled by other books and do not wish to even touch them? This is the Christ Spirit working, directing your learning and guiding you to what you need at the time. Listen to that inner guidance; it is your path to the Light.

The increased presence of the Christ Spirit is manifesting in other ways now. Look to the heavens during the day and at night. There are new configurations of clouds being formed; there are unusual lights in the night sky and these are not necessarily spaceships. The presence of the Holy One creates magnetic variations in the Earth and the atmosphere around it, causing air currents and molecules of energy to react in different ways. This is in addition to the natural changes going on. You are living at a time of great wonder on Earth. Your world is no longer only a world of materiality, but is becoming highly charged with energies from the spiritual world that exist all around it. Become aware of your new surroundings, for your future is one of new beginnings and under-standings. You are the future Light Beings of the universe and you are most loved of God.

Your Light is beginning to shine. We are lighting the flame in your hearts.

The Golden Path

CHAPTER TWENTY-SEVEN

The Increase of Knowledge

By Master Teacher Sananda
1991

This is a time of great tribulation in the world, but also a time of greater joy, for the tides of energy and knowledge are turning and mankind is approaching the time when all energies will be blended into one tremendous pattern of love.

All around you are signs of the coming of the Christ Spirit. The changes you see in weather patterns, ocean currents and the thoughts of humanity are all signs of this coming. In truth, the Master has always been with each soul being, but the actual, full presence of the Christ Spirit will be the culmination of millions of years of preparation for this event.

When have you ever seen such a resurgence of the multitudes toward the churches? When have so many people formed together in groups to study the Word of God and to make the effort to live according to that Word? The inner knowledge and love that each person has always had is pushing outward into full consciousness and will not be denied any longer. If you think this is happening rapidly now, keep watching in the next year and the years after that! Many countries that have had restrictions against religion lifted are seeing their peoples returning in droves to the churches, many for the first time. Those who have worshiped the state are finding vacuums within that should have been filled with high ideals and ideas. They are starting to search for something more and they will find it. All who seek shall find and be filled with the love of God.

Preparations are now being completed in the higher realms for the release of a tremendous amount of knowledge into the world, relating to spiritual and scientific knowledge that will benefit the saving of the Earth itself from further damage. When such knowledge is given by the Creator, it is sent into the ethers, the energy that carries knowledge swirling all about you. Human minds that are open and interested in each separate subject will find that knowledge poured into them in vast unsuspected amounts. Ideas will form, seemingly out of the blue, in those who do not realize their spiritual connections, and "civilization" will take a big jump, even before the end of this century. The electronic wonders you see now will become obsolete in just a few years, as many new wonders take their places.

Channels who are now receiving knowledge from the master teachers assigned to communicate through them will see even more beautiful information flowing and there will be increased pressure to give more time to this service. Although it seems difficult to publish and distribute the written information, the time will soon come when any such information will be eagerly sought.

Those of you who thought you could never learn anything new have an opportunity now to open your minds and find the underlying talents and abilities you have never used. Try anything new and different and you will be surprised at what you can do! Higher energy patterns in the world now and in the months to come will increase the ability of every human being to accomplish wondrous things, mentally and physically. Athletes will find their strength increasing, even without the use of drugs. Scientists will find their knowledge expanding with new insights. Educators will become more eloquent and caring with their students. Writers will have material of wisdom and knowledge popping into their heads. Workers the world over will feel a greater need to do their best and have the strength to do it. Those whose minds are immersed in selfishness, greed, envy, hate and violence will find these traits increasing in intensity, and some will find this so frightening, they will turn back to God.

Be prepared for these internal changes. We are repeating this message many times so that you will not be caught unaware when these new energies cause you to become restless, nervous, depressed or unable to sleep the normal hours you usually do.

For high energy you cannot cope with, take time to sit down, relax and meditate for just a few minutes every few hours. It will calm the energy. Also, remember to ground yourselves every so often. Grounding is simply a technique of mentally sending the excess energies in your body down through the body into the Earth. Mother Earth will absorb the energy, use it, then release it back into the atmosphere and the universe.

You will hear many harbingers of disaster telling of terrible things soon to happen to the world. We do not see them as such. What is happening is the natural course of the continuing creation of Earth and mankind. When lives are lost during Earth changes, sometimes the spiritual selves of these people are fully prepared for that event. Many people continue to live in areas where it is obvious and evident that there will be strong quakes and floods. They do not move away in fear because that is where they are supposed to be and what happens is meant to be, for them. Those who are here to live in future times to rebuild the Earth will find themselves relocating to areas where Earth movements will not endanger them or their families. Those who refuse to listen to inner guidance at all are at the greater risk. When they return to spirit, they will realize their errors.

Those of you who are walking sincerely on the path to Light should not really be concerned about approaching Earth changes or so-called disasters. You know that you will receive guidance for yourselves and your loved ones. If you are meant to be part of the population of mankind to start over in damaged areas, you will be. If not, many of you will provide valuable assistance from the spiritual realm. You are perfectly aware that the body you are using is only an impermanent shell for your use in matter.

You are living in the time of the culmination of thousands of years of preparation. You are seeing knowledge and events that no other race has ever seen. You are the most loved of all races in the universe and will evolve in the next three hundred years to a race of beings that will engulf the entire universe you now know and many others you have no awareness of. Your opportunities and future are absolutely endless and without limitation. You are the children of God.

Our energies surround you at all times. Call on us in your conscious minds and during your meditations and receive whatever guidance and love you are seeking. The power of communication with mankind is ever increasing and you will feel our presence more and more. We send our love and our blessings for your well-being and for your spiritual evolvement.

The Golden Path

CHAPTER TWENTY-EIGHT

The Dimensions

By Master Teacher Peter
1990

Master Peter: We understand that most of those who return to spirit reside in the fourth dimension. When the soul entity rises and becomes the formless being resting and learning in the presence of the Father, does this happen when it progresses into the fifth dimension? Also, please explain the different dimensions and the progressions into them.

The position of the soul entity when it re-enters the spiritual kingdom depends entirely upon its position on the path of Light. Most do indeed enter at the level of the fourth dimension, where they stay until their level of knowledge merits the progression into the fifth dimension. The fifth dimension is one of little form. When those entities who reside there appear to those still embodied, they are usually seen as pillars of Light or just a bright Light. They may project a form, if they wish, to enable the human to relate to them more completely. "Beings of Light" is a good descriptive term. The soul entity has to have acquired the understanding of this kind of existence before it is permitted to enter the fifth dimension.

Remember, as the vibrations of the soul entity increase, the degree of material matter is lessened. When we spoke of the lesser density of the beings embodied in your world later on in time, this is the reason. Eventually, although the soul entities will continue to live on a material world, they will have little form of any kind. They will be known by their vibrations just as those who reside in the upper dimensions are. The world itself will be evolving into a higher dimension of vibration since it is also a living being of a different kind. It will eventually be part of one of the higher dimensions also. A material being, if he or she could see it then, would say that the Earth had been destroyed because it would not be visible to his or her eyes, but it will still be there in a different dimension in time.

The word "density" applies in the higher dimensions just as it does in your world. The dimensions are simply higher layers or planes of vibrations. As the knowledge of the soul entity develops, its vibrations attain a faster rate, thus putting it into a higher dimension. The numbered dimensions are for your benefit and are numbered from one to seven. Mankind is living in the third dimension of time and space.

If a soul entity has advanced beyond the knowledge of the fourth dimension, either in a past life or in the present lifetime, it will proceed directly to the fifth, or even the sixth dimension. This will not be disturbing, because it is well aware of the power and peace awaiting. There are many higher-dimensional entities who have incarnated upon your planet now in order to help with the changes now happening so rapidly. Some have been commissioned to do so; others have requested the "assignment." It is a difficult thing to reduce the vibrations from the fifth or sixth dimension down to the third. It requires a devoted and unselfish need to serve the Creator in this manner.

Can one tell the difference in these people at your level? It is their duty to blend in with the rest of humanity so that the difference cannot be known in any material way. Some of these higher-dimensional entities are born into the world normally and do not recall their mission until adulthood. Others obtain the permission of a host's higher soul in order to merge with one already incarnated in order to serve. People whose higher soul selves have given this permission begin to be able to see things in a brighter light; their thoughts become elevated as to their spiritual destiny and the opening of their inner selves to their inner knowledge. This all happens quite gradually so as not to frighten or disturb the entity in any way. Outwardly, the embodied entity changes drastically in its personality and goals, sometimes to the detriment of the family or other relationships. The career may take on a different pattern of involvement, or a new interest may take over so completely that the person may start training for a new career. This may sound unfair to the embodied entity, but it would not be undertaken if the entity's higher soulself did not see that it would be an advantage to its progression on the path of Light. Working with a higher-dimensional being is indeed a tremendous advantage that advances the host entity many lifetimes.

What then, is the seventh dimension? The seventh dimension is the ultimate goal for all created souls; it is the actual Presence of the Creator. At this level, the soul becomes again part of the actual Eternal and Creative Intelligence that you term "God." It becomes absorbed again into the place it came from. Souls are eternally being created, sent out to learn, and then brought back into the Supreme Being. This is the pattern of the universe, just as everything dies on your planet and then is born again, as the trees, vegetation, animals and mankind. The matter that dies is absorbed into the Earth to create new life again and new Earth to support the new life. All is created and recreated; nothing is still; nothing simply disintegrates. What has been created by the Almighty One never dies, but lives on through the eternal and unlimited ages with the Creator.

Lift your thoughts beyond the material and discover where your path is leading. Untold peace, love and knowledge await your presence. A lifetime wasted in mental poverty simply multiplies the lifetimes of learning you must serve in order to reach the ultimate goal.

Given in the Light.

The Golden Path

CHAPTER TWENTY-NINE

Universal Changes

By the Beings of Light
1993

Alone, of all created beings in the immense system of universes created by the Supreme Intelligence, the planet Earth is now the prime focus of the Creator for the education and evolvement of immortal souls. Over the great millennia of the past, many other planets in your universe have had this distinction and have either evolved to much higher dimensions or finally met with extinction, their basic matter being used again.

The planet Earth is a body of matter on which spiritual beings are incarnated for the purpose of evolving into higher planes, or dimensional frequencies, in order to raise their vibrations closer, ever closer, to the Living God of all things. The planet itself is also changing its dimensional frequencies; the surface and all things upon it are evolving, rapidly now, into different patterns of life and consciousness. Changes occurring on the crustal continents of the world are but an outward indication of the vibrational changes occurring within the planet. High energies surrounding the Earth, fluctuating constantly, provide the planet with the different elements of energy that are needed for this transformation.

People are feeling this ongoing transformation deep within their beings in the form of pressures, anxieties, the need for creativity and excitement and, most of all, awareness that there is something very powerful within them that is shouting for recognition! The ultimate realization of each soul entity's real and vital identity as an immortal spiritual being is the most exciting and meaningful experience any human being can have. It is the beginning of human life on a new plane of understanding, self-confidence, security and love of self. If you have not experienced this, let us help you come to this realization.

When your soul was created (and creation is an eternal and ongoing pattern of the Ultimate Intelligence you term God), a part of that Intelligence was given to your soul. Everything that is God is also a part of you. This realization has tempted many people to run around, shouting out loud, "I am God!" That was a real turn-off to the religions of the world, for, used in that manner, the meaning was sacrilegious. No created soul is the totality that is God, but every created soul is a part of that totality. It would be better to shout, "I am a part of the Living God!" or "I am a child of the Living God!" for even though all particles of living energy are linked together in that totality, the Supreme Intelligence is ever the First Part of all creation and the Ultimate Source of all. It is this Ultimate Source that all soul beings are yearning to return to and become part of.

Many groups now recognize the Biblical name of God as "I Am," and have incorporated those words in their own identities to mean that they are an integral part of the Supreme Intelligence. This is pleasing to us, for it denotes an understanding of the relationship each soul has to God. Very few people now actually believe that God is a white-bearded old man seated upon a golden throne, surrounded by legions of angels and saints. Mankind has now progressed, for the most part, from the need to personify all unseen things into the images of men or women to the understanding that the Supreme Intelligence is the ultimate form of the energy that creates and is a part of all things. Every atom of energy or matter is infused with the presence of that Intelligence. That is why all needs, all prayers are heard instantly and acted upon instantly. Thought in the higher dimensions is sent more quickly that the human mind can comprehend and assignments are given to spiritual beings of Light to arrange what is necessary to give assistance in ways that are beneficial to each soul. Human minds think they have all the answers, but their answers are but the musings of an infant. The Eternal Ones see far beyond the mind and can see what can really be accomplished in that life that will further the intentions of fulfilling the original purpose of incarnating into matter.

Life purposes in your present time are, for most souls, very deep and important. The soul beings who are fortunate enough to incarnate at this time are trying very hard to learn lessons that incorporate deep mental and physical suffering in order to reach understanding of the meaning of these emotions. The wars and misery that you see now all over your planet are part of that mass intention of learning and they will continue for a long time yet. This is not to say that you must turn your backs and ignore the needs of such people, not at all. Give your aid, your work, your prayers for the suffering, while understanding why they are going through this. Ask not that the wars cease instantly, but seek to send strength, understanding and faith to those in such dire circumstances. That is what they need now. Food and supplies for the bodies are not nearly as important as the spiritual insight that is most urgently needed. Word is now slowly leaking out to the world that there are cores of deeply spiritual people banding together in areas of terrible hardship. More and more are finding peace and strength deep within themselves when there is nowhere else to turn. That is the ultimate purpose of the suffering. Truth must be learned the hard way for those determined to break down the barriers of self- aggrandizement and greed. Those who do not succeed in their purpose during this lifetime will be sent to other planes of existence to learn again and again, until they come to their awakenings.

This is not a time of fear or uneasiness, but a time of self-searching. Start slowly, if you must, examining the way you think, how you feel about yourself and others, finding the deeper good intentions and the shallow faults that have been absorbed by the constant sights and sounds of civilization. Examine your thoughts to see how much you have been "brain-washed" by the sexual themes of the media and the biased yam-merings of racial extremists. Deep within you know that all mankind is a part of God, that all mankind are brothers and sisters and need to find each other and care for each other. Erase the differences and find the common factors that every person carries as his or her inheritance from the Creator. All basic needs are the same, regardless of the race or culture. Love is the common denominator that brings all things together. Love is the very essence of the Supreme Intelligence and is present in every atom of life, part of the very air you breathe and part of every cell of your body. When you deny it or ignore it, you are denying your very own basic existence, and the negative vibrations denial causes in your minds and bodies bring on the terrible diseases that so plague Earth today. When all is in harmony in the mind and consciousness, the body responds by being harmonious and healthy also.

Seek out the inconsistencies within your thinking, your beliefs and the way you live your daily life. Human life today needs to be lived with enlightened thought and intent. No longer can one who is consciously on the path to Light wander through life in a haphazard manner, taking things as they come. There is purpose to life, and that present purpose for all mankind is to consciously prepare for the inner changes that are happening, to have full awareness of the physical changes in the body and in Earth herself. Be aware of your inner beings and constantly listen for the guidance that is being sent to each one of you to help and prepare you for each change as it occurs. You are in no way alone in all of this; your every step is counted and guided. You are loved by every being created by the Eternal One and are watched over constantly. You are most precious beings to all of us and the Eternal One enfolds all of us with unrelenting love.

Amen.

CHAPTER THIRTY

Discernment

By Master Teacher Peter
1990

Along the way of developing your knowledge of the inner being who is your spiritual self, there are many potholes to fall into. I am speaking more precisely of the many so-called New Age practitioners that abound in every city today. These are the people who, for the most part, are very high souls have found out they possess a psychic ability of some kind and are very busy making a living from it. These are the ones who have not found themselves spiritually and many of them do not even bother to delve deeply into their own inner beings or help their clients to do so. "Readings" are mostly about human affairs, trying to find what the future holds, what wonderful man or woman the client is going to meet and so forth. The readers are able, most of them anyway, to tap into the fourth dimension and are clairvoyant enough to be able to see future events and receive messages from those willing to communicate from that dimension.

For human beings who are consciously and faithfully trying to proceed along their spiritual path, contact with or reliance on readers of this kind can be very confusing and disappointing. A lot of information gained in this way does not coincide with the teachings of the higher-dimensional beings and the resulting confusion pulls many away from their studies entirely. This is very sad. Although we try very hard to send the right signals and guidance, the channel is sometimes closed in our faces and the soul entity who was going to accomplish so much in this lifetime either turns its back on the acquiring of spiritual knowledge or waits a long time before trying again.

It is extremely important that you look very carefully at the people whom you turn to for teaching. If they are unknown in your community and seem to be drifting from one place to another, they probably have not gained the wisdom to find their places in the world nor have they much real guidance in working with people. If you decide to take a reading from someone unknown, tape record it carefully, then listen to it again when you get home. Use your inner wisdom to decide if the words have validity or not. Do they really relate to you or could they be just a "stock" reading that could fit anyone? If events are foretold or past-life events seen, keep them on record and put them away. Wait for someone else, totally unrelated to the first reader, to find the same event. Verification is important.

Finding a teacher or guru for the purpose of a one-on-one relationship in a long-term learning process is becoming impossible. Not for the reason that the teachers do not exist, but because there are so many more who wish to be taught now, which is as it should be. A great deal of teaching is done now within small groups of people, studying and learning together. If such a group has an outstanding and learned teacher to lead them, they are indeed fortunate. Make the most of what you have, and always be looking for deeper knowledge, wherever you find it.

Yes, there are many, many highly spiritual people who are doing readings professionally and these are being done with the need of the client foremost in the mind. This kind of professional psychic will help the client deal with personal problems as well as teach some important truths he or she needs to deal with. Again, record the session and review it often to see if the knowledge given is right for you. We are communicating with many spiritual people today and giving them knowledge to share with others. Only your inner wisdom can tell you if the truth is being spoken; you must learn to discern the false from the true.

All of this is being given in order to help you deal with the very confusing events soon to transpire. Your American government is finding fraud and stealing among its own members and those who are honest are trying very hard to do something about it. Those in power all over the world are doing the same thing. Greed has become commonplace and taken for granted in most parts of the world, which has left the world a very ripe fruit for the picking. There are those who will put up marvelous fronts and promise all sorts of returns from investments made with them. Be very careful. Reliable investments are going to be few and far between; the financial situation in all nations is unsound and, in some cases, breaking apart. You will be hearing of this more and more. Be especially aware of psychics trying to tell you of great opportunities; they may be working for the fraudulent financiers. Be careful of what you have; you will need it later when things become more difficult financially.

Leaders in the East are going to become very powerful and will begin to have great influence in world markets and financial centers. The leader who has been foretold in your Bible as the "Beast" is very active now and is busy gathering followers and making his presence known. He will do many things that will look as if he is the one to solve all the problems, but instead he is working behind the scenes to amass billions of dollars with which to set himself up in power. When you begin to read of this "wonderful" leader, be very aware of who he really is. The Light Workers of this world must train themselves to sense the false statements and know enough not to involve themselves in organizations that promote the "Beast," of which there will be many. *The organizations will have the word "flower" in them in some way; by that sign you can recognize them.* Keep yourselves close to the inner Christ Spirit and ask for help if you cannot tell or are not sure of what you are hearing. Open your channel to listen and the truth will come through.

There will be many who will be deceived and will suffer for it in one way or another. Form close ties with others who are on the path to Light; keep the Light around you, especially when there are unknown pressures coming to bear.

There are high souls embodied now who are slipping into governments all over the world in order to expose and defeat politicians who are being used by the dark forces. Listen carefully to what is said by these politicians, and you will soon recognize the Light Workers among them. Support them with prayers or any other way that is needed. The coming years at the end of this century are crucial for all peoples of the world. How the challenges are met will make all the difference in how severe the Earth changes will be and whether or not the world will be immersed in global warfare. It need not be.

Above all, follow your inner guidance; make time, and I mean *make time,* for prayer and listening for inner guidance. It is important now as it has never been. Be aware of all that is been given. It will protect you and help you in all ways and at all times. Ask for the help of your angels, spiritual helpers, the Christ Spirit and, above all, your Supreme Creator. Help will be given.

God bless you all.

The Golden Path

PART TWO

BIBLE STORIES
REVISITED

Genesis

By Master Teacher Peter
1990

This is the time to speak of things that have been hidden from mankind since their entry into solid matter. Much of what I will speak about has to do with soul migration into your world.

When the Creator decided to spread Its influence over a wider span, there was a separation made of Itself. The first separation was the creation of a spirit being who would be a recognizable power, separate, yet one with the Creator and of a slightly lower and denser vibration. This spirit being was to be the generating power of all creation in the many universes to be created during the span of eternity. This being you are aware of as the Christ Spirit. After many thousands of years of your Earth time, the Christ Spirit created separate soul entities out of His own vibrations and endowed them with free will so that they would be able to develop their own personalities and intelligence. They possessed awareness of universal knowledge, yet they were free to form their own ways of thought and to travel where they wished in their vibrational forms. After many, many eons of time, many soul entities became interested in the solid matter that the Christ Spirit had been busy creating in many parts of the universe, using the energy of the Master Intelligence you call God to solidify that universal energy into stars and planets.

One of the planets, Terra (or Earth), was developing into a beautiful green planet with living foliage and a different atmosphere. This was something not seen before, and soul entities were desirous of traveling to this planet and experiencing this new experiment in matter. The Christ Spirit complied with their requests, with the restriction that soul entities must keep their identities and return back into spirit intact, as the new planet had not been fully completed as far as life forms were concerned. Solid bodies, in the form of animals, were created at first to provide vehicles for the soul entities to inhabit. There was a great rush to enter these animal beings, as there were not too many of them. Their forms were not then as you would think of animal life. Many walked erect as well as on three or four legs and some were endowed with a capacity for intelligence. As time went on, the desire to experience a solid way of life became so intense that those in solid form were pushed to multiply the species they inhabited to provide more room for other soul entities.

Human-type bodies were eventually introduced into areas on the planet where life could support them and these forms became the most desired by the soul entities because of the bodies' ability to manipulate the sticks, stones and other building materials that were needed to construct shelters for these beings. Attention began to focus on the material world they now lived in; awareness and connection with their Creator became dimmer and dimmer. The new dimension the soul entities were surrounded by presented the difficulty of having to pay constant attention to finding food and safety, which left little time to spend in the state of worship that they had always known in spirit. The memory of their higher-dimensional beginnings became dim.

Sex itself in material beings of every kind was a fascinating new experience for all of those embodied, and this was indulged in beyond, far beyond, the intent of the Creator. Soon, there were cross-matings between animal and human species that produced very odd shapes and forms. The Creator looked down on this and saw the confusion His soul entities were making for themselves and decreed that thenceforth no such mating could produce a living being. His command to cease the cross-mating was strong and most of the soul entities, encased though they were in their own human minds, heard their Master's Word and drew back to their own species.

There has been much written about beings of odd proportions, part animal and part human. Word of this came down through all the centuries of oral and written history and is now regarded as myth. Almost every myth of mankind had its beginning in the distant past, no matter how unlikely the stories now seem to you.

The Christ Spirit finally improved the human stock and, as in your Biblical account of Adam and Eve, brought the new strain into a beautiful part of the new planet which is now referred to as "The Garden of Eden."

This area was populated eventually not by just one man and woman, but by many thousands of beings whose soul spirits had been especially chosen to inhabit the new race upon the Earth. They were given every beautiful thing they could desire, every kind of food they could think of, every beautiful animal to keep them company. By this time, animals themselves were not inhabited by the soul spirits of the Christ, but by a legion of newly born soul spirits who were created for this purpose. Their understanding was limited, as they are today, and they existed with an inborn instinct and comprehension given to each new type of animal as they were created by the Master. Most of the animals were simple, gentle creatures who came to the humans in the Garden for companionship and protection.

The snake in the Garden was not an actual animal, but the representation of what is now known as the Devil, Satan or the dark forces. During their first entry into matter, there were a number of soul spirits who were angry when they could not enter matter in the way they wished, angry at the restriction on sex, angry that they should have any restrictions at all. Yes, there was "war in heaven." The Master Intelligence, or God, resolved the conflict by sending these spirit souls into the far reaches of space, there to remain until they might come to realize their errors. When the last species of mankind was created to live on Earth, these wayward souls were given the choice of staying where they were or being sent to Earth, where they must stay until the end of this age. At that time, if they still have not learned the ways of love, they will be entombed in a place by themselves until they do. These wayward souls have been on Earth ever since and comprise the dark forces that mankind has had to contend with and protect itself against. They are the forces that seduced the humans in the Garden to listen to their dark and resentful thoughts, to long for things that were forbidden.

When the Christ Spirit saw that His new race was being contaminated by these thoughts and desires, He forced them away from the Garden and destroyed much of it. The many varieties of animal life that dwelled there were scattered over the Earth and given the means to take care of themselves. The area that was the Garden has died and been reborn many times (that is, the land area has sunk into the ocean and been raised up many times) and is now part of the land area known as Syria. The exact spot will never be known because of its total destruction. Nothing important could be gained if it could have been recognized. The importance lies in the truth that mankind forfeited their easy life and were forced to live as they do — to work for a living and to be totally responsible for themselves and their actions. This was called the Fall.

There are many writings regarding the actual creation of the human body. The theory that other-world beings "seeded" the Earth is not true, despite the claims that other-world beings are making now. They do not say these things to lie to you; it is part of their own mythology and has been misinterpreted. The seeding was done by the Christ Spirit. The first seeding was mankind. Other seedings created different and intelligent beings on other planets in other galaxies. Mankind went through many different experiences, many times becoming so corrupt and sinful that the Earth was wiped clean and a new race with a new set of soul beings was again seeded. Your scientists are finding many types of skeletons now, being directed by spirit to do so, but as yet have not understood that these were not descendants of prior races, but different races entirely. It is not permitted for me to tell you how many races there have been, because it makes no difference to you now. These races rose and died out before your final human race, as you now know it, was created.

You are probably wondering why other species from galaxies beyond yours seem to be so much more advanced and are coming here to help *your* advancement. They were indeed seeded after your first races evolved, but were of a different reality. That is, their conceptions into material beings were made only once, and their minds raced ahead to take the lead in many galaxies in order to set up the cooperation of all species in the universe to be ready for the final evolution of the human race. There is much still to be said on this subject and much that has been written. This is your challenge: to search for the final meanings of all this.

Today, the human race has progressed and learned and become a source of great pride to the Christ Spirit, in spite of the hatred and wars that permeate your world at this time. The Light of the Christ Spirit in human souls is getting brighter every day. This has caused those who have invited the dark forces to dwell within them to work even harder to influence those who have not come as far on the path to eternal knowledge and it is they who are causing the darkness in your world.

There is a total balance in the universe of positive and negative, as you well know. This holds true in the very atoms that comprise your material world and all vibratory systems. Good and evil are also vibrations that must be balanced until the end of this age. So do not be terrified of the evil you see and hear. Those of you who have the interest to read this are learning that you are a child of the Christ Spirit and that part of His spirit resides in you. You have the knowledge, the creativity, the power that are part of the Christ Spirit. There is no reason to fear the dark forces as long as your own conscious mind is aware of this and holds fast to the truths which are within you. You may have heard the instruction to "hold the White Light about you." This is simply visualizing a bright white Light coming down from above, entering your body at the top of your head, then beaming out all around you to form a barrier against all dark influences. That barrier is the force of love, against which nothing can prevail.

That is not to say that you will not have harmful or hurtful experiences. You have to experience these things in order to increase your knowledge. The schoolhouse, as your world has been called many times, is still a place of learning, of advancement. Solid matter has been provided to create a source of difficulty, hard work and the need to withstand temptations that abound every day. The Earth is a place to finalize each soul spirit's learning, especially now at the end of this age. Welcome the experiences, no matter how hard they may be, for you know they will give you precious knowledge and eventual victory over the challenges. A soul spirit who refuses to learn will have to go back to the beginning and start all over again, with full knowledge of the past and of its failures. This is really the "hell" you speak of, not a pit of burning fire. The fire is the symbol for the eternal agony of defeat and disgrace. The final warnings are being given to all mankind, NOW!

It is most important that you, as teachers, healers, helpers of every kind, do not hide your Light under the sofa. It is true that truth cannot and should not be forced upon people, but eternal truths must be made available to all who will listen. Many are now searching for this knowledge and will instinctively seek you out, not knowing why they are doing so. Do not fear that you are without the ability or the knowledge to teach. When speaking to others, ask first for the Christ Spirit to guide your thoughts and words, and it will be so. You will be surprised at what will come out of your mouths, directed by your inner knowledge.

These words will cause doubts at first, but when the seeds are planted, they will come to harvest in many, many people who feel the void within themselves and who are really searching for the truth. Give your friends and strangers at least the chance of progressing. Those who know the truth and keep it to themselves when it is asked for will suffer for it. *To know the truth is to teach the truth.* The Christ Spirit and His angels are "waiting in the wings" to help you with this effort. Open your mental channels and accept what you feel and, in some cases, hear. Eventually, you will even feel "pushed" to do things of which you are fearful; do them.

You will be happy and filled with an inner Light when they have been accomplished. Love is surrounding you now in a way that has never been on your planet before. The Christ Spirit wants to call His children home.

God bless you all.

CHAPTER TWO

The Chosen People

By Master Teacher Peter
1990

Back in the time of recorded Biblical history, a small tribe of people lived who claimed descent from one of the sons of Adam. They were a peaceful people, living together in isolated groups so that their strain would not be diluted by breeding with other tribes. They kept the Word of God as best they could and knew how to, setting up a rigid priesthood to see that the laws were kept.

The tribe grew into many thousands of people, spreading into the northern part of Asia Minor and around the Mediterranean Sea.

When Egypt grew into great power, they were seen as a convenient source of labor, so were herded together and sent into slavery. The Jews, as they were then known, were used to build great edifices for the Egyptians and as house slaves. They were treated very badly by the haughty Egyptians, who considered them lazy and stupid, especially since the Jews insisted in worshipping only one God, when everyone "knew" that there were many gods that had to be placated in order for life to run smoothly! Still, the Jews never relented and kept the knowledge of the truth in their hearts.

When, finally, Moses led them out of Egypt, the Jews' happiness and relief was almost unrestrained and it took quite a while for Moses to organize a system so that the long trip on foot would not be dangerous or completely unstructured. Food wagons were put together of the combined supplies from all the people; water supplies were apportioned throughout the large group so that all would have access to it when needed. Wagons were set up to use for the ill, and those who were skilled at nursing were sought out to stay with those wagons. Many small wagons and carts were pulled by the people themselves, although they had with them many oxen and other cattle that were pressed into service more and more as the days wore on. The older and the ill people rode when they could, but there were not enough carts to hold all of them and many died in the first week of the long trek.

Word had come to the Jews through their prophets that they were to be given a beautiful land of milk and honey, which they called the "Promised Land," and now the time had come to find it. Moses had a heavy load on his shoulders; he had to lead thousands of people through a completely barren wilderness, trying to keep order and to bring as many through as possible. Then he had to find the "Promised Land," which, at first, seemed a complete impossibility.

Why did all this happen at all? Why was this group of people singled out for such hardships and condemned to march for so long, just to find a decent place to live?

First of all, the Creator had a plan, a very long-range plan that was to go on for many centuries. The Jews were chosen to implement this plan, as they were the only people left on the Earth who still remembered where they came from and were trying to retain communication with the Most High. It was time for a great testing, to see if these people could keep their beliefs under the worst conditions and constant derision of their faith. The testing in Egypt was terrible, but the worst was yet to come.

Moses was a high soul sent into matter to be their leader and also their teacher; he was a part of the testing process. When their energy and spirits were low, he, being constantly given inner guidance and knowledge, found water and food for them that was provided by the Creator. It was not an easy time for Moses either, for, as a man, he had many doubts about his abilities to do what he was commanded to do and he suffered as much as the rest from hunger, thirst and the strain of the exodus. When all seemed lost many times, the Inner Voice would instruct him what to do and he obeyed. If he had not obeyed or had doubted that Voice, all would have perished. The education he had received at the royal house in Egypt served him well many times and it was for this that he had been sent there. The plan of God had started long before and many people were unknowingly a part of it.

The testing continued and when Moses was instructed to go up onto the mountain to receive the Laws of God, it was very hard for the people to simply camp and wait. They were tired, hungry, and wanted to just go "home" and be done with this awful journey where nothing grew and wild animals plagued them at night. They could not understand why Moses had deserted them to roam in the mountains for so long and became restless and angry. They were easy prey for those who remembered the gods of Egypt and, since they could see nothing, hear nothing or had nothing to cling to for security, a few of them who had lost their faith urged the others to build a god out of what metal and gold they had brought with them from Egypt. They felt that their One God had deserted them and now they needed another; they needed a god who would listen to their prayers and take them to the Promised Land – now! So the golden calf was made. The people responded by throwing aside their religious restrictions, the laws they had so long obeyed and respected, and went wild. The Jewish priests and those who still believed in and served God were afraid for their lives and retreated quickly into clefts in the rocks at the base of the mountain for safety. Some of them were found, tortured and killed, being blamed for the misfortunes the people were undergoing. All was in turmoil.

On the mountain, Moses was deep in meditation and completely unaware of what was happening. The presence of God filled the air and the very rocks themselves. The laws written on the rocks were not produced as the movie showed, immediately and dramatically, but one at a time a rock was detached and shaped before the eyes of Moses. The letters formed slowly and with great force so that Moses would become aware of them as the truth they contained was poured into his deepest conscious thoughts. It was a time of learning for Moses, as well as of the physical forming of the tablets. This took many weeks and Moses was in a meditative state the whole time, being fed energy by God to keep his body alive.

When Moses finally gathered together the heavy tablets of stone, having been given the energy to carry them, he slowly found his way back down the mountain, still surrounded by spirit and the joy of what to him was the greatest miracle ever seen by humankind. It was in this aura that he came to the spot where he could see the mass of the Jewish people dancing around an idol. He could feel the vibrations of anger, wild thinking and desires and was shocked to the core of his being. He cried out to God and asked how this could be when God had just given them so much! The Creator knew what was happening, of course, and told Moses that the tablets must now be destroyed, that the Jewish people would have to earn the right again to be in possession of them. With a broken heart, Moses threw the tablets down the mountain in front of the people and thundered at them that they had sinned and denied their God!

The silence was almost unbearable; the people came to their senses and realized what they had done. The longed-for Laws of God written by the very Hand of God lay smashed to pieces at their feet. Those who dared crept forward and put their hands on the stone fragments; they were burned. The fragments retained the power that had been poured into them but it was now forbidden to the Jewish people. Most of them fell to their knees and asked forgiveness in great agony of soul and conscience. The priests came forth from their hiding places in great sadness and also put out their hands to the tablet fragments. To their hands a great power and peace was felt and the priests gathered up the pieces and stored them away in a chest. They could not bear to leave such precious objects exposed to the elements.

Then the Almighty spoke to Moses and told him that the Jewish people would now have to continue their wandering for many more years as a punishment for their failure to keep the faith, and Moses had to tell this to his miserable people. Try as he might over the years, he could not find a land where they could rest and find peace. God sent them in circles many times, in hard and barren places where there was no water or food. They had to eat what grasses they could find and many times it was given to Moses to find water for them. Those who had started out from Egypt died and only their descendants were left to keep going. The lesson learned at the mountain was never forgotten and parents taught their young the truths and the faith that was to sustain them all those years.

What happened to the tablet fragments? When the people finally all returned to faith in the knowledge that God had given them, direction was given that a special chest be built in which to carry the fragments. The gold that had been formed to build the idol had been melted down and carried with them so that they would have a source of exchange in the new land. Now they were told to melt it down again and transform it into a beautiful chest to contain the Laws of God. They were happy to do this as a way, finally, to prove their devotion to the Almighty. The making of the Ark took many months, as most of the talented metal workers and carvers from Egypt were gone, and only remnants of their craft were known by their children. When the priests were directed to remove the fragments from the chest where they had been kept, they found a new miracle. The fragments had formed back into whole tablets and the Laws of God were now as they had been in the beginning of their creation. The people were filled with elation and wonder and were eager to press forward to see and touch them. Suddenly, thunder sounded, and a great voice was heard that told them that they were not to touch the tablets or the Ark, that the energy within the tablets was so powerful that it would kill any who dared to touch them!

The priests were allowed to place them in the Ark, but even they felt a tremendous power emanating from the tablets. The cover of the Ark was put into place, and there was silence once again among the people. How then, were they to take the Ark with them? Finally, poles were made from what was left of the carts they still had, and rings were carefully welded onto the Ark, without human hands touching it. The poles were inserted and they went on their way. It became a great honor to be one of those carrying the Ark and it took the strongest among them to do it.

When the people were finally allowed to reach the Promised Land, the Ark was kept in the temple they built for it and revered as a holy thing of God.

Over the centuries, the Ark was moved many times and is, today, hidden in a safe place, away from the wars and evil that have invaded the world time and time again. It will not be revealed again until the world has gone through the hard times it faces now, when the Laws of God on the tablets He gave to humanity will be renewed, never again to be hidden away.

The wanderings of the Jewish people taught them that keeping the Word of God is not easy and they learned to keep and respect it with love and thanksgiving. They became truly the Chosen of God, living together in love and harmony.

Again, there was a testing. Now the Roman Empire became the power of the world and, again, it found a peaceful, unresisting people to use for its own purposes. Again, the Jews were pressed into service and into slavery. This time, they did not relent; they refused to worship the gods of the Romans. The testing was successful and the time had come for the Creator to send the Christ Spirit into flesh to teach them in person the higher lessons now to be learned and to give them the faith and hope they needed so badly in those times of oppression. They now were deserving of the great miracle of life.

Jesus, the Christ, spoke to probably ten thousand people during His time on Earth, which was but a small portion of the population of the then-known world, but His words of life and hope spread quickly from town to town, country to country and as far as a person could travel in those times. The teaching was not given just to the Jewish people, but to all who would listen and try to understand. To many Jews, there was resentment at this; they felt Jesus belonged to them alone, that He was their Saviour and no one else's. Did He not come to bring them out of their terrible predicament? The priests of the Jews by this time had the people pretty well under their thumb and, like the religions of today, built in many of their own laws in order to do so. They did not appreciate a carpenter from a miserable little town preaching about a spirit within the person whom the individual could listen to and obey. Many of the Chosen knew in their hearts that God was within Jesus and left their homes and jobs to follow Him all over the country so they could listen to His teachings and learn more about the Kingdom of God. However, there were many who simply wished to get rid of Him so they could get on with what they wanted to do; He was a danger and an impediment to them. Thus, finally, the Gentle Carpenter was crucified.

After the Risen Christ completed his visits and teaching of the disciples and those to whom He appeared, He materialized in many other places on the face of the Earth where word of His coming had not traveled. In many cultures there is written evidence of His presence and teachings. In primitive cultures, He simply taught them the rules of living and love, since they had not evolved to the level of understanding anything further. He was much loved and revered by all who were privileged to be near when He taught.

This part of the Plan of God had been completed.

Over the many years since the Christ went back into spirit, the Jewish people have been looked down upon, enslaved, tortured, killed and simply regarded with distain since the entire race has been blamed by humanity for killing the Christ. Is this fair? Of course not.

Although the Jewish people as a whole today do not accept Jesus as the one in whom the Christ Spirit embodied, they are a very faithful people to the Laws of God that they were entrusted with and they adhere to them devotedly. The Creator does not condemn these people because their ancestors could not accept Jesus. Remember, Jews in the time of Jesus had traveled over much of the then-known world and were used to many different men claiming that they were the Messiah. They knew that to make a mistake and follow a deceiver would bring disaster to them and their children; they could not afford to do this. Those who had not heard Jesus, the Christ, speaking in person had only heard tales about him. Although it sounded good, there was still the fear in their hearts and, in the end, they wanted to rid themselves of a threat. This was so, even though they believed deeply that a Messiah would come. A humble carpenter was just not their idea of a Messiah. They expected a powerful man, decked out with precious gems and expensive clothing, who would overthrow the Romans and set up a new empire for the Jewish people.

Great expectations are still one of the downfalls of the human race.

The Chosen People

The Creator is the most understanding of fathers, and He understood what had happened and forgave those who could not believe and receive what had been given. Truth has been given to the Jews in many other ways and their knowledge is considerable and not to be looked down upon. The truth regarding Jesus, the Christ, will be gained when each soul returns to its home.

Humanity, on the other hand, has been most cruel. Some Christians have decided that only they have a right to the advantages of their belief; that anyone who does not believe as they do will not gain the glories of Heaven and sit at the Right Hand of God. Each different religion seems to have their own version of that. Eastern religions are just as selfish; their God is only for them. How foolish. There is one Supreme Creator containing all knowledge, from whom all things were created and all intelligence given.

Antisemitism, as it is now called, is rising again in Europe especially, the place where the Jewish people have seen so much hatred and been so despised. Instead of trying to show kindness to the Jews to make up for what has happened over the past century, it is becoming fashionable, again, to make them scapegoats for every difficulty society encounters in rebuilding the nations of Europe. Now it will become, again, the fault of the Jews that all this happened. Unbelievable!

Not until humans, each one of them, can truly understand in the heart that each soul entity bears the responsibility for its own actions will this unjust cruelty cease. Until then, people will still insist on putting the responsibility for any unwanted or unpleasant event on someone else. The Jewish people have always been the scapegoats for modern society, so why not use them again?

Beware. The Creator of all has not condemned the Jews. Those of you who do condemn them will incur a very unpleasant karma. Those who have, in past lives, despised, harmed or killed Jews because of failing to take responsibility for their lives are now living as Jews themselves and will feel the brunt of the evil intentions of man. Do not ever forget the admonition of the Christ: "What ye shall sow, ye shall reap!" This is universal law; you cannot turn your back on it.

In your Bible, it is said that the sins of the fathers would pass on to their children. It did not say that it was the Will of God that it be that way; it was seen that mankind would place the blame and carry it through the centuries.

Respect all peoples, all nations, all religions. We are all a part of the Family of God and the Creator surrounds All His children with love. Can you do less?

Given with love.

The Golden Path

CHAPTER THREE

The Essenes and the Dead Sea Scrolls

By Master Teacher Sananda
1991

Y ou are asking about the Essenes and I will give you a history of the sect and the part they played in the coming of the Christ and the Dead Sea Scrolls.

When the Jewish priests, over many centuries, had laid out the required activities and beliefs for the Hebrew people, restrictions on everyday life had grown to a point that many people felt their personal freedoms were being impinged upon. Some of these people were extremely spiritual and understood that many of the restrictions were not asked for by God, but invented by the priests in order to have a tighter control over their worshipers. At that point, a large group of Hebrews began to form a secret, separate group, setting down carefully the Laws of God as given in the Old Testament scrolls they possessed. They found these laws to be sensible and easy to follow. Being human, however, they too created a number of rules that would apply to their own sect. They felt that to keep their group pure in thinking and pure in body, tight laws of living would need to be set. These rules of living are quite well known today, so I will not repeat them here.

When the group was ready, its members spread out in the cities and villages to talk to others who they felt would be interested in becoming a

165

part of their new community. Many men came back with them and the Essenes were born.

At first, very quietly, the Essenes acquired large homes on private tracts of land adjacent to the several cities near Jerusalem, where they set up separate small communal living sites. At these homes, the laws they had conceived were put into motion and tried out. A few laws were tossed out because they were too restrictive, but in the main, the laws of living were found to be satisfying to the membership. They effectively kept the focus of living on the spiritual studies they wished to immerse themselves in, without the outside worries and distractions of everyday life.

Now, the Jewish church finally heard rumors of such a break-away sect operating somewhere and were very concerned about it. They wanted no interference or opposition to the laws they had set up and were enforcing, lest the general populace would want to break away from the Temple also. Finally, now that the Essenes' existence was known, it was not too hard to locate their communal centers. Intense pressure was put upon the Essenes to abandon their new beliefs and come back to the Temple, which, of course, they refused to do. When these pressures became a constant irritant to the Essene students and teachers, they began to look for a place to live where they would no longer be a threat to the Temple and the priests would not harass them any longer.

They sent out scouts to find new locations, and found that anywhere near even small villages they were hounded by the local priests to move on; they were not wanted. They sought farther out and away from the inhabited areas and eventually came to the conclusion that they must find a site in the desert in order for them to dwell in peace.

The ruins at Qumran are not the ruins of the Essene community, as has so long been believed. They are ruins of a Roman encampment that was used as a type of jail for Roman officers who had stepped out of line. It was quite luxurious and comfortable for the time. There were several sites on which the Essenes camped at first and then they built small walled-in communities for themselves. They were not master builders like the Romans, and their buildings were just barely sufficient for their needs. Emphasis was on raising their awareness of spirituality to be closer to God and His angels. What ruins there were disintegrated centuries ago.

The Essenes grew in numbers and in strength. They were known far and wide as the most spiritual, wise, honest and kind people of their time. They gave unselfishly of themselves and their goods, sharing with each other and with any and all who were in need of help in any way. The Temple had given up at this point and simply tried to keep the worshipers they had, ignoring any mention of that "rebel" sect.

The rules about women and sex are pretty well-known. It was acknowledged that man had strong needs and desires, some stronger than others. Those who felt they must be with a woman were given leaves to do what they needed to do; then they returned to the restrictive life. They were much ahead of their time, realizing that men and women had the gift of free will and that no priest or leader should interfere with that right. Sometimes, when a real love match was made, the woman was brought back to the commune, and separate housing was created for the couple. They did believe, however, that in order for a marriage to be consecrated, a child must be born. Three years were given for this to happen. If, in that time, the woman proved to be barren, she was given food and what money was available and sent back to her people. It was not understood in those times that women had the same spiritual being and intelligence as men, which was sad. When a married couple did have children, the family stayed in the commune and the children of such couples were raised according to the Essene ways and laws. The children were considered communal property who belonged to the whole commune. This was not entirely a bad idea, as they were showered with love and teaching from everyone. There was never a child who felt left out or less than the others.

Now, what did Mary, Jesus and John have to do with the Essenes? Mary's father was an Essene. He had married her mother when she became pregnant, and they lived for awhile in an Essene commune. After a few years, the little family felt they needed to live more in the world and they withdrew from the commune to live in Nazareth. Mary's father never gave up the Essene ways, however, and most of their home life was based on the restrictive laws that he followed. He made regular trips back to the commune to renew his beliefs and studies.

When Mary was about ten years old, the Essenes were deep into the studies of the prophecy that a Messiah was to be born to the Hebrew people. The Messiah was to be a being who would show humanity the way of life and renew communication with the divine ones. There was a select group within the Essenes who had developed their minds to a point where communication with God's Holy Servants was being made quite regularly. They were told about the projected coming of a Holy Being and that this Being's spirit would reside in a human man that was to be born for this purpose. It was given to them to make the choice of a pure young girl to be the mother of the male child. The Essenes, of course, never even considered any but the female children of the Essene groups and began their examination of the little girls. A certain age-group was given that they should adhere to. Mary and several other little girls whose parents lived away from the commune were also brought in and examined by the teachers. Notice, the word "priest" is not used in conjunction with the Essenes. There were none. All were equal in the sight of God and each man taught and learned from the others.

The decision that Mary would be the one to bear the Holy Child was made. Her family was brought back into the commune, and they felt very honored, needless to say. Mary was given special lessons by the teachers to prepare her for the coming event, as directed by the Holy Beings they were in contact with. It was realized that, because of the customs of the time, she would have to be protected by a husband and live in a normal situation when the time came. The man who was to be the physical father of the Holy Child was also carefully decided upon. Joseph was of the lineage that had been decided upon at the beginning of time for the Holy Child to be descended from. His family also had direct contact with the Essenes, but were not entirely a part of the sect. Joseph was approached and asked to come to the commune for a time. He had no idea what they wanted, but it was deemed an honor to be asked. He was treated with respect, taught by Mary's teachers of the prophecy, and was included in the times of communication with the Holy Ones. His whole being was infused with the love and increased knowledge that he was being given. When the time came to inform him that he had been chosen as the physical father of the Holy Child, he was overcome with thankfulness and humbly accepted the responsibility that was to be given to him.

Joseph was many years Mary's senior, but he was a man who was well-established in his village and much respected. He would be a man who would give Mary love and protection.

They were finally introduced to each other at the commune, and each liked the other immediately. Mary, at this time, was thirteen years old and beginning to bloom with womanly fairness. Joseph went home but made regular trips to the commune to visit with Mary and to study what was taught to him. Mary continued to grow in grace and beauty, fully understanding what was eventually to be.

The time came, when she was nearing her fifteenth year, that she and her family were sent home to live in Nazareth again. There were other children in the family by that time, and not all were happy to be separated from the commune, although they had been prepared for this. Only Mary and her parents knew of her destiny and sometimes she felt quite alone. As planned, Joseph began visiting the family, and when it was deemed the right time, he asked for Mary for his wife. When the mother and father assented, the first step of Christ's entry upon Earth had been taken.

An angel did appear to Mary soon after this; it was not a vision but an actual transformation into fleshly being. The angel was clothed in a shining white robe, surrounded by the holy white aura. It did not have wings. I refer to the angel as "it" because angels are neither male or female. Mary knew immediately who the being was and knelt in wonder at its appearance to her. The angel announced to her that the coming of the Holy Being was imminent and that Joseph had consented to be the father of the human baby. She was given instructions as to the physical union to come and how to take care of herself. She was also assured that no matter what happened within the minds of the villagers concerning her, all was well and the angels would be constantly around her and Joseph, giving their love and encouragement.

Joseph and Mary were betrothed according to custom. During this time the custom was that the man was allowed to visit the woman to become better acquainted with her, but no physical contact was allowed.

The writers of the scrolls that were included in your Bible really did not fully understand the conception of Jesus. Joseph and Mary, because of their society's customs and pressure, could not admit to the fact that they had conceived the child themselves. When it was learned that Mary was with child, her parents stoutly defended her and said that Joseph had not touched her. Joseph had the hardest time, because the responsibility of sex was upon the man. His family and friends wanted him to get out of the betrothal and turn his back on Mary. Of course, he could do no such thing. He had followed the instructions given to him for the conception of the baby and was not troubled in his heart about it. When the furor died down and it was finally accepted by both of the families that they were to be married anyway, Mary and Joseph began to live together as husband and wife and were accepted as such.

The forced trip to Bethlehem to register for taxes was as it is reported in the Bible. It was not reported that the Romans made it a terrible experience for the simple villagers. They were prodded and whipped in some cases simply for the pleasure of the soldiers. Unless the villagers had brought enough water and food with them, on very short notice, they were half starved when they got there. Only those who had large amounts of money with them were able to buy lodging; the others slept where they could and bought what food they could from what little was for sale. It was a time of terror and immense stress.

Joseph and Mary, being forewarned of the event, had enough money for a room at the inn and plenty of supplies to see them through. Joseph's family traveled with them, but they were separated during the march. It was a shock to Joseph to find that all of the available rooms had already been taken, just at the time when Mary was so close to having the baby. She had ridden most of the way on a donkey, but was extremely tired and in pain from muscle cramps because of the long ride. Joseph almost "came unglued," as you might put it, shouting and demanding a place for Mary, at least. His shouting was heard by the woman who lived at the inn, the innkeeper's wife. She looked out and saw Mary's face and felt pity for her, as she had just had a baby herself not too long before. The innkeeper's wife slipped out and took Joseph's arm, guiding him away from the entrance. She told him that there was a cave behind the inn where they kept their animals; it was dry and warm and that perhaps they could clean away a space for the night. Joseph at first was a little unhappy about this idea, but had no choice. The innkeeper's wife went with them to show the way, holding a small lantern. There was fresh hay set aside, and they used it to make beds for Mary and Joseph. She left the lantern with them and returned to the inn.

The story of the birth of Jesus is well known and accurately presented in the Bible. Further information is presented in Chapter 4.

Now, John, called the Baptist, was also an Essene who lived at the same commune where Mary was taught. He was part of the select group who received communication from the Holy Ones and his role in the life of Jesus was given to him shortly after the birth of Jesus. He was indeed a cousin to Jesus and the families were well-acquainted. John saw into the future and realized the sacrifices he would have to make and the death he would suffer at the end of his ministry. It gave him a rather fatalistic view of things, but there was no hesitation about accepting, with all his heart, the path he was to follow.

When Jesus came of the age when he was to receive the Christ Spirit, John left the Essene commune and began to preach, heal and baptize all those who would come and listen. He shouted the announcement to any who would listen that the Son of God was to enter into a human being and teach the word of God. When the fascinated people began to follow him around, priests forced him away from the cities and communities where he was teaching, so he retreated to the nearby desert valleys. He found stream beds where he baptized those who understood what he was saying and wanted to be part of the new Kingdom of God, as they understood it to be. His voice was intense, and despite his appearance, which was extremely wild, humanity was drawn to the love and power he projected. He was indeed a "voice in the wilderness."

The Essenes and the Dead Sea Scrolls

Jesus came to John there, in a desert stream bed, and received the Spirit of Christ into his mind and body.

Did Jesus really die on the cross? Yes.

The Dead Sea Scrolls are now being read and interpreted by many different people from many different points of view.

The Dead Sea Scrolls were written by the Essenes of many different communes and also from many different points of view, according to their own backgrounds.

It must be understood that many Essene communities did not believe that the select group in the one commune could really communicate with the Holy Ones. They rejected completely the Holy Birth and the teachings of Jesus, the Christed One. In fact, they taught that belief in such teachings was heresy, thus putting themselves on the level of the Hebrew priests who did the same thing. There were many writings about Jesus during these years, both by the Essenes who helped to bring about the birth of Jesus and by Essenes who were so blinded by their own tight beliefs and restrictions that they turned their backs on the Son of God and wrote what they thought to be the truth.

After the Christ had ascended to the Father, controversy raged on between the different factions of the Essenes, to the point that they carried the battle of thoughts into the very temples they had broken away from. The disciples were just beginning to teach on their own, but were wise enough to travel away from the villages where they had been born or were living during the time of the Crucifixion. The Romans finally became very angry about all of the bickering going on in the Hebrew communities and decreed the extermination of all Essenes. The brothers and sisters of the communes received a little advance notice of the edict and hurriedly abandoned their communes, blending into the throngs of the cities where they quietly continued their ways in small groups for many, many years.

Before they left, however, the scribes, determined to hide the scrolls from the Romans, gathered up the libraries of scrolls, wrapped them in skins and put them into jars to preserve them by whatever means they had available. Members of several different communes climbed into the hills where there were small caves and pushed as many of the jars into the openings as possible, then filled the openings with loose stones. Others found other hiding places. Although many scrolls have been found, know that there are whole libraries still to be discovered, some in good condition, some completely obliterated by time.

The writings contain the beginnings of today's Bibles, given to some by divine thought, and they contain universal laws and truths. Some writings found were written by those who were the unbelievers and who wrote what they thought had really happened.

Do not be upset by what these scrolls contain. Listen to what is given, listen to the different interpretations that the present professionals are coming up with, but listen with the discernment of your inner being as to the validity of each pronouncement. You will know what is true and what is not.

There are several intact scrolls in the possession of collectors which contain very beautiful writings about the beginnings of Christianity, describing the Resurrection of the Christ. Those who own them do not realize what they contain, only that they are rare and valuable. The scrolls may or may not eventually come to light.

The birth and life of Jesus were planned shortly after Earth was created, recognizing that humankind would need instruction in the laws of spirit during its progression in time. This soul was given the honor to be embodied as the child Jesus. This soul has not embodied again into human form, but has had the responsibility of teaching those in human form who have attained the ability to listen. This soul now channels (as it is known now) truth, love and wisdom to many, many people, this channel being one of them. It is indeed a high honor and one no spiritual being who is allowed to do so takes lightly. We are all children of the Eternal Creator of All and delight in whatever service we are asked to perform. The Christ Spirit remains as the Creator's highest and most powerful voice in all the universes and under whom all souls have their being. Those who worship the being Jesus and who do not understand his relationship to the Christ Spirit are missing the blessings they should be receiving in this life. The Christ Spirit taught humanity not to pray even to Him, but directly to God, the Eternal Creator.* All things come from this Supreme Being and are shared with all created life on your Earth, on all planets, in all universes. All things are a part of that Eternal Creator and It is a part of all things. Prayers are always received, understood and acted upon because the Holy Ones are a part of all energies that surround you as the ocean surrounds the fish in the sea. Nothing goes unrecognized or unheard. Nothing is ever lost. Everything that is created, whether it be physical being, actions or thoughts, remains forever in the vaults of eternity. Remember that when anger stirs your mind.

We are here to send you knowledge as you request it. It is our great honor to so do. We send you the blessings of the Eternal Spirit to guide your lives now and in the spiritual kingdom you will return to.

Amen.

---

*Luke 4:8

CHAPTER FOUR

The Story of the Birth of Jesus

According to Master Teacher Peter
1991

Alone in all the universes are souls that exist in order to prepare the way for spiritual beings to transmute their energies from the spiritual realms into the physical realms. These beings are very close to the Creator of all things and are highly revered and respected among the most highly developed souls of the Hierarchy. Sananda was the first soul of this type created and remains the closest to God of all subsequently created souls of this nature.

The Supreme Intelligence foresaw from the beginning of the creation of your world that mankind had a long way to climb before there would be enough intelligence to understand their spiritual origins and be able follow universal laws that apply to all parts of the spiritual realms and all material universes.

The soul first created from the Mind of God is and always will be the highest manifestation of the essence of that Creative Intelligence. It is "He" who is indeed the Creator of your planet and universe; it is He who has projected a part of His Essence into each created soul in order to be able to send love and guidance to those still in the spiritual kingdom and to those embodied on Earth. From that Source of all Knowledge come the wisdom, strength, love and guidance that every human being would be totally lost without, even if he or she does not realize it.

That Totality of Soul is, of course, the Christ Spirit.

When humanity had become advanced enough to know the difference between good and bad, had grown to revere and seek power and wealth, to enslave one another and kill their own brothers and sisters, it became time for the Christ Spirit to step in to renew the teachings and laws that had been set down for humanity many centuries before. The laws that had been given were supplemented a great deal by mankind in order to control groups of people. This was done not only by Jewish priests, but also by religions the world over. Basic laws of living have always been evident because of the circumstances that occur when they are broken. Not only did the laws themselves need to be clarified, but for many of the peoples of the world, the concept of universal love had never been encountered and was sorely lacking in the hearts of humans.

Sananda had been chosen by the Christ Spirit to enter the body of a man in order to bring forth an Earthly being who would consciously understand the mission he had undertaken. It was his responsibility to take care of the body of Jesus, to educate the conscious mind in all the available knowledge of that civilization and to prepare the mind to be able to accept the incoming spirit of the Christ to live with Sananda in that body. The human consciousness of Jesus was to be preserved as a carrier to take care of the Earthly necessities so that the Higher Consciousness of the Christ would be free to take care of His people by teaching, healing and giving His all-consuming love to all those about Him. It was not easy for the man Jesus to accept these things, but his inner spiritual knowledge was very open and the realization of the importance of what was to come was always present in his mind.

When the time came for the entrance into materiality, Sananda came forth and the young woman Mary was chosen by the Essenes, who had been given the responsibility for choosing the mother. The father of the human child was also chosen, an older man who would be able to protect the child and teach him the ways of the world in wisdom and love. This man was Joseph. There was no need to fertilize Mary with divine sperm; there was an adequate supply available there in matter. This myth of divine insemination was created by humans in order to more fully generate the belief in Jesus as the Son of God. Mankind felt Jesus could not truly be the Son of God if Mary had not been impregnated by God. Human minds were not able at that time to fully grasp the concept of spiritual incarnations and the full meaning of them. That myth is found in many old religions for the same purpose.

The Story of the Birth of Jesus

I will repeat and expand upon some information that has already been given to this channel.

The Essenes were, at that time, the most highly developed spiritual human beings on the Earth. They had separated from the Jewish Church and kept to themselves in separated communities based on communal living. They studied the word of God and there were those who had constant communication with the Christ Spirit. It was by this communication that the command was given to find a pure-minded, spiritual young woman, still a virgin, who would be the mother of the human child. Mary was chosen, her family being members of the Essenes, and she was sent home to await the circumstances to follow. Soon, Joseph was chosen and sent to ask her family for her hand in marriage. The family was quite pleased at the choice. Mary had other siblings in her family, but they were not aware of what was to transpire.

Mary's personal guardian angel was chosen to announce to her that it was time for the child to be conceived and gave her instructions as how to care for herself and the child when it came. Mary and Joseph were not married yet, only betrothed, and it was not considered proper for them to even touch each other. To have sexual relations at that point was considered a sin. However, Joseph had also been instructed that in God's eyes the single sexual act with Mary to create Jesus was a holy rite and was to be treated as such. After that, Joseph only saw her occasionally, as the rules of conduct at that time prescribed.

When Mary's condition become obvious, there was an uproar among her relations and Joseph was urged to break the betrothal, as they did not know who the father was. Mary's mother and father, of course, understood what had happened and staunchly defended and protected her. The furor died down after a few months, as such things always do, and Joseph and Mary were quietly married.

As the months of the pregnancy wore on, Mary became more and more aware of the spiritual presence that would be incarnating into the fetus of her unborn child. It seemed to speak to her and quiet her fears and concerns for the child. Joseph also felt the presence and this created a bond among the three of them that will last through eternity.

When Mary was near the end of her ninth month of carrying the child, the Roman government decided to tax the Hebrew people even more than they did already and sought to accomplish this by instituting a drive to record every Hebrew family on its rolls, so that all could be taxed. Each family had to travel to the city where their family roots were planted, or at least had originated. Joseph was of the lineage of David, as prophesied, and his family was required to travel to Bethlehem to be counted and recorded.

When this news came, Joseph was greatly agitated because of Mary's condition. Wives were required to make the journey also, and he was fearful for Mary's life and the baby's survival during such a long and arduous trip. Mary calmed him down and told him that she knew that she and the baby would survive dispite the hardships that might be involved. She was so much a part of the miracle by that time that negative thoughts or fears could not reach her. So they packed the money and supplies they would need and started the journey. The family of Joseph was also included in the trip, though they were far advanced in age. The entire group had thus to travel slower than many others and arrived in Bethlehem long after dark, after most of the others from their village had already arrived.

In the milling throng of hundreds of people, Joseph's mother and father had become separated from them but, strangely, Joseph did not feel concern. He knew that they were being taken care of. His concern was for Mary and the child. He understood how important it was that the child be born safely into his and Mary's keeping.

As soon as they could, Joseph and Mary rushed to the only large inn in Bethlehem to get a room. Mary's labor pains had started and Joseph was frantic. The innkeeper gruffly told Joseph that the inn was filled to overflowing, that there was no room for any more and then closed the door. Joseph was stunned and felt utterly helpless in this situation. The door opened again and the innkeeper's wife appeared with her finger to her lips and softly told him there was a cave behind the inn where their animals were kept. It had been cleaned for the occasion of the many guests the innkeepers knew were coming. Perhaps there would be a space they could clear for Joseph and Mary to sleep for the night. She had seen Mary's condition and felt sorry for her.

The innkeeper's wife led them to the little cave and showed them where there was a pile of freshly cut hay. Joseph cleared away a space and piled the hay into a bed for Mary and covered it with his traveling cloak. During the middle of the night Mary gave birth to the baby, with Joseph helping her. As is true for men today when they are allowed to assist in the birth of their children, the bonding with the baby was just as important to Joseph as it was to Mary. The birth was fairly fast and easy.

The Story of the Birth of Jesus

The story of the "Wise Men" in the Bible is accurate as far as it goes, but the church fathers, in the time when the Bible was reconstructed, left out many details. The Wise Men were astrologers, as you understand the term today, men who had studied the skies most of their lives and knew that a great event was about to happen. They came from different parts of the country and were not about to miss out on what the stars foretold. Did a star actually appear and lead them to Bethlehem? Yes, of course it did. Such an event was too important for the Father of All not to mark it clearly for all the world to see. It was not an exploding nebula, a comet or a spaceship. It was an extraordinary event of nature to pinpoint the appearance of the baby Jesus. Do you think God was unable to do such a thing? Mankind still wants to put all events in nature into neat little packages and exclude the idea that the Creator of all dimensions could go against the natural flow of things by placing such a star in the sky.

The star itself had been in existence for several weeks before the birth of Jesus, and the astrologers had been on the road for quite a while by the time they saw that its path halted over Bethlehem. Suddenly, they saw a great light shoot down from the star directly onto the area behind an inn. Then they knew their search had ended. They were rather disappointed on seeing a baby wrapped in a homespun blanket lying in a donkey manger. They had expected something quite grand and wonderful. When they came closer to the baby, however, they felt the vibrations of a great being and understood at once the significance of what they were seeing and feeling. They presented their gifts in a ritual appropriate for a king and felt that this moment was the fulfillment of all their years of study. The Wise Men camped there beside the cave the rest of the night, then started back to their homes the next morning.

During the night, as the Bible states, they were warned to go back another way, as the Romans by then had received word of the birth and the unusual star. They were aware of the old predictions of a Messiah being born in Bethlehem and were afraid that this might be the child who would overthrow the empire.

There were many shepherds watching their flocks in the hills surrounding Bethlehem. At that time of the year, they lived with their flocks and guarded them against the wild animals in the area. Most of them were asleep when the great star appeared in the sky, but awakened when the brightness of the light shone over the hills. They wondered if morning had come and were confused for a time. In the starry heavens above them, they heard singing — a chorus of many voices — becoming louder and louder. As they gazed up in wonderment, three angels appeared as in a mist, and told them in voices that echoed over the hills that the Messiah had been born in Bethlehem and that his name was Jesus. They pointed the way to the shepherds and broke into beautiful songs of praise to God and the miracle that had occurred.

The shepherds were obviously paralyzed with fright and collapsed on the ground during most of this heavenly announcement. When the angels gradually disappeared and the night was quiet again, the shepherds came to themselves and checked to see that all of them had seen and heard the same thing. Then the excitement grew and they realized it was real and it had happened to them! As fast as they could run, they flew into Bethlehem and shouted the news to all they met as they searched for the little cave. By the time they arrived, it was nearly sunup and the Wise Men were packing their gear for the trip home. Mary and the baby were sleeping and Joseph was stirring around, helping the Wise Men. The shepherds, recognizing that it must be the place because of the presence of such richly dressed visitors, drew near to the mother and child and immediately felt that they were on Holy Ground. Many others had followed them to see what the commotion was all about, and each knelt in wonder when they came near the little family. By dawn, there were hundreds coming to see the baby and give homage.

The Romans, however, soon dispersed the crowds and herded them into the lines required for the recording of names. Joseph took Mary and the baby and quietly slipped into the line, putting their names into the rosters; then as quietly they slipped away onto the road leading back to Bethlehem.

Before Joseph awakened that morning, he, too, had been warned not to return by the same route they had taken to Bethlehem from Nazareth, as the soldiers would be searching for a newborn and mother. He was very upset at the thought of danger for Mary and Jesus. It took a great deal of courage for him to finally realize that they could not return home. The voice in his vision of the night before had instructed Joseph to travel with his family to Egypt, there to dwell until the danger would be past. Egypt!! They did not have the supplies for such a long trip and Mary was still weak and tired from the journey and the birth! But the command, he realized, was from God and there was to be no questioning such a direction. Joseph understood finally that they would be taken care of and protected, and so the long journey began. It was hot, and the sparsely traveled road was barely a path, strewn with rocks and low-growing cactus plants. Mary rode the little donkey they had brought with them from Nazareth with Jesus in her arms, dozing now and then. For Joseph, the walking was hard and they seemed to cover so little of the distance each day. By night they camped beside the road, hoarding their supply of water and food. Joseph was instructed to find new food supplies from the desert plants and thus they were able to survive the harsh conditions.

Finally, they reached the Nile River and followed along its shores for many miles. They had heard that Elizabeth, Mary's cousin, lived somewhere in the region, but they had no idea just where. Joseph was guided by inner spirit directly to the home of Elizabeth, where they were expected and happily received.

Joseph, Mary and Jesus lived there beside the Nile in Egypt with Elizabeth and her family until Jesus had attained the age of five years.

Now, Joseph was aware that the education of Jesus must begin soon and that he must return to the Essenes so that Jesus would benefit from their teachings. He worried about this in his heart until one night near morning, a vision from God came again and announced that it was safe to return to Israel. Joseph rejoiced and awoke from his sleep to waken the others with the news.

Mary was very happy where she was and was shaken with the realization that their happy, comfortable existence was to be shattered and another long journey begun. Still, she knew what must be and accepted it. That day was busy with packing and putting together the supplies for the trip. This time, they would not need to forage in the wilderness for food. The trip home was uneventful and they were welcomed back to their family home in Nazareth.

Joseph immediately enrolled Jesus into the Temple school so he could be trained in Hebrew and the Torah. After two years of this training and the training he received from his father as a carpenter, Jesus was introduced to the Essene Community which had been anxiously awaiting his presence among them. The Jewish priests knew only that the hours Jesus spent with them had been cut and they were unhappy about it but could not get past Joseph's stern insistence that Jesus must be at home more. The Essenes were still in secrecy because of the priests' disapproval and did not wish to raise an issue by letting them know Jesus was being given Essene training.

Jesus was not required to become a full Essene, with all of the restrictions they required of themselves, because it was realized that this being had work to do in the world and was being prepared for it. He was introduced to the highest spiritual teaching they were capable of and it was not long before Jesus' memories of his spiritual being returned and entered into his conscious mind. He absorbed all that he was taught and soon came to understand the mysteries of the Torah that the priests had no knowledge of. Jesus could not help showing off a little at the Temple, talking about his newly found knowledge in terms that the priests found astounding, which made them rather uncomfortable, to say the least.

When Jesus reached the age of fifteen years, he began to feel the restrictions of his surroundings and knew that there was more to be learned elsewhere. He talked about this with Mary and Joseph and finally convinced them that he must be free to somehow travel to other cities and places. They were poor people, and his parents had no means by which to send him on such a journey. One day, Jesus saw a camel caravan winding its way through Nazareth and followed it to a market where the camels were being unloaded. He sought out the leader of the caravan and plied him with questions about where they had been and where they were going. When he found out the long distances the caravan traveled on a continuing basis, he rushed home to tell his parents about it and asked if it were possible that he might join the caravan so he could accomplish the traveling he wished to do.

At that time, caravan people were not too highly regarded. Many of them were thieves who would steal in one town and sell in another, and they were not to be trusted. Mary and Joseph had protected Jesus all his life and were afraid to let him be exposed to such people. They finally went and talked to the caravan leader, at Jesus' insistence, and found him to be a kind man, even though he was very wise to the nature of mankind and one who put his hands on as much money as he could. They explained to him that they had no money, but that their son wished to travel with him. The caravan master liked the boy Jesus, but didn't wish to feed an extra mouth. Jesus was quick to detect that some of the men who had come with the caravan were nowhere in sight and suggested that if they did not come back, he could work in their stead. The caravan master considered this and told him to come back in the morning to see if there might be a place for him.

Mary and Joseph knew in their hearts that this was indeed the time of separation and spent the night preparing Jesus' clothes and food for the trip. The mother's heart was full of tears but also full of pride that her blessed son was doing what he was committed to do. In the morning, Jesus left with the caravan as a full working member.

Working a caravan of camels loaded with heavy boxes and parcels, walking most of the time and guiding the camels, was not an easy job. The heat of the desert combined with the rough language and manners of the other workers nearly drove Jesus to his knees at times, for he was used to the love and gentleness of his own family. It took some time for him to harden to the life and to retain his own gentle ways, regardless of the taunts of the other camel drivers. During the long treks, there was time to think on all that he had learned and to relate it to the real-life circumstances he was experiencing. At night under the desert stars, the voices of the angels and the Master Teachers spoke to him and taught him. He was never alone.

Jesus left the caravan after three months and took ship when they reached the Mediterranean Sea. He paid his way by working on the ship and traveled all through the Mideast in this way. He learned from the wise men he found and taught others what he had learned. He left many footsteps that extended much farther than mankind has realized all over that part of the world.

His teenage years were years of discovery of himself and the world in a physical sense, which was a wonder to his spiritual self. As he grew into his 20's, his wisdom and gentle strength were much sought after by those who had heard of him.

When he reached his 29th birthday, the spirit of God appeared to him and guided him to turn his footsteps back to Nazareth, for the time was coming close when the Christ Spirit would enter into his body and mind, as had been foretold.

Two years after that, Jesus walked into the wilderness to find John the Baptist and received the Christ Spirit into himself. Thereafter, He was to be known as Jesus, the Christed One.

The story of that occasion is told in the following lesson, "The Entry of the Christ and the Crucifixion."

Today, the soul entity Sananda teaches through many people embodied on Earth and follows the directions and guidance of the Holy Spirit of God in his work. The man Jesus died and is no more. His memory is not to be worshiped. The Christ Spirit who used that body is still the same and directs the energies and creations of your universe as its highest expression of God. Even so, the Christ Spirit is not God. Jesus, the Christ, tried to make that point very clear when he told his followers not to pray to him, but to the Creator of All, using his essence as a go-between only.

The reality of the Supreme Intelligence and Love that are God surrounds every created being at all times, being the very substance of life. Direct your prayers to God alone, knowing that they become part of that substance, part of God, part of the Christ Spirit that works within you. You are never alone and what you need will always be granted to you in ways that will be to your best benefit, when you ask.

Become aware of that wonderful presence within and let it guide you through your lifetime in matter; use that strength and determination to fulfill your purpose in life and to help others find and fulfill their purposes.

The Christ Spirit has always been with each of his soul children, but His essence is coming into the world now with much more intensity as this era comes to a close. Much has been said about the "Second Coming" and some say, "But He never left!" That is true to an extent, but the full presence of the Master has not been felt on Earth since the creation and when that presence is fully manifested, there will be no question about it! We are not given the manner and the time when that will happen, only that it is happening very gradually in this decade and will continue to expand in the next one hundred years.

The expansion of this presence is what is triggering the inner need in the hearts of humans all over the world to search for the spiritual side of themselves. The old stories of comfortable religions are not enough anymore. Those searching for the truth will find you. Teach them what they ask, a little at a time, so they can absorb the "new" concepts they will be learning. Those of you whose purpose it is to teach have a great responsibility now and your Master Teachers are there beside you with all the guidance you will need. Indeed, the Christ Spirit is on Earth again, teaching the word through His soul children.

Love and blessings to you all.

Dear Peter: As recorded in St. Luke 1:26-35, the virgin birth of Jesus is laid out pretty clearly. I am going to be asked why your version of the birth and that of the Bible do not concur. It is very seldom that your teachings and those of the other masters do not agree with Biblical accounts.

Ruth, it is true that the Bible was written long after these events took place and that the writings were mostly divinely inspired so that the truth would be told correctly by the writers. However, the new religion by this time was taking hold very rapidly and the recounting of what happened was being asked for from all sides.

There was also a great deal of confusion and reluctance to believe that a heavenly being had been born by a human being. The writers of the Gospels knew that the reality of incarnations could not be understood by the people of this time, so they used the old "holy conception" myth to underline the fact that the Christ Spirit had indeed inhabited the body of Jesus. There are only a few accounts in the scriptures that were invented for this purpose and this is one of them. Readers of this information must make a decision as to what they want to believe. Those who have progressed along the Path will be able to search out the answer to this question within themselves, where they will find the truth. As more advanced knowledge is released to mankind, there will be other discrepancies between the communications and the Bible and they, too, will have to be determined in the heart of the student.

The Golden Path

The Entry of the Christ Spirit and the Crucifixion

By Master Teacher Peter
1990

There was a day, above all days, when the Prince of Peace allowed Himself to be hung upon a cross in full view of His family, followers, disciples and the soldiers of Rome. Why did He do this?

The Christ Spirit was the first soul created by the Father of All, so long ago that your minds could not conceive of the time span. It was taught by the Creator to know all things in all ways down through the untold centuries of time and space. It was the Creator's First Servant, Messenger and Creator of Planets. Other souls were created much later to be the "office staff," so to speak, of the Hierarchy of the Universe, those who would oversee the education of trillions of souls to be created to fill the vast reaches of the universe. souls of the Hierarchy were taught by the Christ Spirit; they were and are directly under His care and direction.

When the new souls were being created, the Hierarchy put them into order and began their education. It may seem that they came immediately into the Earth plane, but that is not so. Their education took many thousands of centuries before they were ready to think clearly and be able to use the free will the Great Father had given them. The teachers of the

Hierarchy continued the souls' development until they were ready to be on their own. This advanced many of them to the thought that they could set up their own hierarchy and rule themselves in the way they wished; the soul Lucifer was their leader.

When we speak of War in Heaven, it was not like your Earthly wars; it was a tremendous conflict of power that encompassed the entire universe. It was then that the power of negative force was born, and it developed into a wall of soul/mind power that devastated the peaceful aura of the Kingdom of God. It lasted about a thousand of your years, which is but a second in universal time. The Lord of All would not allow this to be and sent those who had defied Him into the empty places in space to rethink their actions.

Soon after this, the Creator felt it was time to give His created souls a place to further their education and commissioned the Christ Spirit to create the solar system that you now inhabit.

The Christ Spirit formed the Sun and the planets much as your Bible states, except that the "days" mentioned were thousands and millions of years. When all was in place, the Earth itself was formed.

When mankind had lived and developed on Earth for many centuries, they became very self-centered and refused to listen, as they had been taught to do, to the Father of All. They ignored the inner voices of the Christ Spirit and their teachers. Again, the Christ Spirit was called upon to help and teach the embodied souls. Not once, but many times and under many names did the Christ Spirit come to Earth as a human being for this purpose. Your people who study religions have recognized that great teachers came to Earth every thousand years to teach, which precipitated new religions. The Teacher came and taught the basic truths of the universe and how to live in a peaceful and loving society. Humans created religions.

The story of the birth of Jesus into the world you have read in Chapter 4.

The child born of Mary was named Jesus, as had been planned, and the child grew and was nurtured by Mary and her husband Joseph in Nazareth. From about the age of three years, Jesus had full knowledge of who he was and why he was there; he was to be the entity who would be engulfed and merged with the Spirit of the Christ to be the Supreme Teacher to the world, whose teachings would live forever. This was a great responsibility and he was well aware of it. As he grew to adulthood, the thought of this responsibility grew heavy and, human as he was, he almost dreaded the time when the Christ would come.

As the time grew close, the Christ became very near to Jesus and spoke to him often in his mind, giving him love and courage so that the transition would not be so traumatic. The gentle pressure of His coming to Jesus was not to be denied.

Jesus had been hearing a great deal of his cousin John's teachings in the wilderness and felt a great need to be there, but, for some reason, held back. One day the way was opened and he knew the Christ Spirit was ready to become one with Jesus. He packed a small bag with some food and water, told his mother that the time had come and departed to the wilds of the desert where John was preaching.

It was a long and hot journey, walking over rocks and climbing up and down hills and gullies. When he finally heard the excited voices of others who were also traveling in the desert, he knew that they were also going to hear John. He did not join them, but followed at a distance.

Finally, there, through a dip in the hills, he saw and heard running water — a small desert stream — and there was John. John was surrounded by about one hundred people, standing by the side of the stream and sitting on the sloping banks. He was preaching about the coming of the Messiah, that the time was very near when He would appear. John interrupted himself every now and then when a person would come into the water and ask to be baptized into the belief.

Jesus watched John all through the hot and muggy day, waiting for the moment when he would be called by the Christ Spirit to approach John. When the sun was low and almost hidden by the barren hills behind them, the call came. There was no hesitation, no going back. Jesus descended the slope where he had been resting and walked down the bank of the stream to John.

John looked up, stopped in the middle of a sentence and simply waited. Jesus stepped into the stream where John was standing and greeted his cousin. John knew this was to be the Messiah but had not really expected him to be Jesus.

Jesus knelt before John and asked to be baptized, which surprised John, but without a word, John baptized Jesus.

When Jesus rose, his hair dripping with the muddy water, there was a different feeling of urgency in the air. Suddenly, a beautiful white dove came flying down from the sky and landed on the shoulder of Jesus. A strong and very beautiful Voice came from everywhere and announced, "This is my Son, in whom I am well pleased!" The dove cooed and pressed its head to the cheek of Jesus, then flew away.

Every living thing in the gully where the stream was flowing was quiet; the feeling of the presence of God was upon them. Jesus stood quietly, but His inner soul was soaring with the experience of becoming one with the Christ Spirit. He finally turned and embraced John, who was still speechless, then walked away down the gully and up into the hills of the arid wilderness.

John turned to the people when Jesus had disappeared from sight and told them that this was the Messiah; this was the Great One they had been waiting for. All who were assembled and were a part of the experience came into the water to be baptized, whether they had believed John before or not. When all had received John's blessing, they departed to their homes. John gathered up his few belongings and began the long walk to his own home, far away, for his work was finished. He had prepared the way and the Christ had come.

Jesus walked a long way, then sat down to rest. The blending of the Christ Spirit with his own soul, although a very advanced and learned soul, was difficult and exhausting. The Christ was merging into every part of His being and raising the body's vibrations very quickly. Jesus was becoming a supreme spiritual being clothed in the flesh of matter. The higher vibrations tore at His nerves at first, then made Him feel like flying! His mind was seeing and feeling things He had never even imagined, for He was beginning to see through the Christ Spirit's higher consciousness. The forty days in the wilderness were almost a torture, but had to be endured in order to become in truth the vessel of the Christ Spirit.

The spirit of the dark forces taunted him endlessly, trying to get him to deny the Christ Spirit, to keep the Christ from incarnating into a human form, but to no avail.

The Christ Spirit and Jesus became as one. Jesus retained his conscious being, but gladly and reverently sublimated it entirely to the Christ. The love of Christ and the love of Jesus combined to create a beautiful aura around Him, which was felt by His family and all people who came near.

Jesus, the Christ, taught, as written in your Bible, and touched humanity as he had never done before in all the previous incarnations. Humanity had evolved to a point where it could understand much more of what He was teaching, although He still had to put universal laws and truths into very simple, story-like language. When He was confronted by the Roman military, He simply drew a cloak of invisibility around Himself and walked away.

Jesus, the Christ, was greatly saddened by the conditions, cruelty and want endured by the Jewish people and tried in every way that He could to help them. Yes, He could have turned the whole situation around and made the Jewish people the rulers of the world, had there been that intention. But He knew that this was not to be, that the Jewish people, as well as all other peoples of the world, had to learn to accept the truths themselves and live their lives in the way they had determined before incarnating. Human beings still had to understand that theirs was the power to change their world; God would not do it for them.

The disciples of Jesus, the Christ, were souls on a similar level to that of Jesus, and they had incarnated for the purpose of working with the Christ during this time. Until Jesus, the Christ, came and asked them to follow Him, they had no memory, but at that moment, all knowledge was returned and their mission understood. That is why they dropped their nets, left the money-changing table and so forth without question, without hesitation.

When the time came that the teaching of the Christ had come to an end, He gathered the disciples together at the Last Supper and told them that He would be returning to spirit. They understood, but the human part of them cried out and begged Him to stay. The soul that was Judas cried out in his mind, for he loved Jesus and the thought of what he had to do was almost too much. He had no choice. When Jesus, the Christ, told him to go, he went to the priests and betrayed the Christ.

There was still human feeling in Jesus, the man; he knew what was going to happen and was terrified. When Jesus, the Christ, prayed to the Father of All that night in the garden, it was Jesus, the man, fighting against the Christ Spirit with all his strength, who asked to be relieved of that experience. The Christ within understood and let the prayers of Jesus rise to the Father without stopping them. As the night passed, the presence of the Christ Spirit and the loving Arms of the Father quieted the being of Jesus so he understood, at last, that the Father's Will must be done.

Why did Jesus, the Christ, allow Himself to be treated in such a manner? Because although His teachings had spread far and near, and He knew that His disciples would spread them even further in that time, He also knew that a belief could become very thin for a people who could not see a Messiah or touch Him. Something had to be done that would be so miraculous and wondrous that it would never be forgotten. To let Himself be whipped and ridiculed, crucified (the worst way in the world to die) and then to come back to life again were circumstances that no human being could ignore. And, of course, He was right.

There were many lessons in the crucifixion. The Christ was teaching His beloved people that the mind and the spirit can overcome anything

Earth can hand out. Appearing before His disciples and followers after His resurrection showed them that the death of the body is not important, that there is an eternal spiritual life waiting for every being. This was something the people of that time were not really sure of. Christ proved it.

"Into each life some rain must fall," is an old saying. If it did not, there would be little purpose to become embodied in your dimension. Know that no matter how hard the rainfall, there is always an end to it. It is up to you to shield yourself by the knowledge you gain from studying the words of the Christ and listening to the inner wisdom that is sent to you from the Christ Spirit and His messengers. There is no reason to fear the storms of life when you know you are surrounded by the angels of God. There is so much love around you. All you have to do is accept it, live by and with it and give it to others. In your lives, that's what it's all about.

God bless you.

CHAPTER SIX

The Resurrection

By Master Teacher William
1991

At this time, we will discuss the question of the Rising of the Christ from the tomb. Did this really happen? Most certainly. Not only had Jesus, the Christ, promised his disciples this would happen, but the Christ Spirit Himself had planned to demonstrate, by this reversal of nature, the real essence of the spiritual beings He had created through the Supreme Creator. This Holy Plan had been formulated during the creation of your world. The realization that human beings would never be fully able to understand the principle of eternal spiritual life without a fully recognized resurrection was the reason for it.

To make sure this truth was fully imprinted upon the minds of His followers, a small group of angelic beings waited at the empty tomb for the first to come who would see the opened door. When Mary of Magdala and several other women came because they wanted to be near their Lord, the angels shone forth in all their glory and announced to the women that the Christ had burst the bonds of death and had risen from the tomb and the regions of death. The women were nearly overcome with fright and amazement at this, to them, miraculous appearance. When they recovered their senses, the tomb was dark once more. They rose to their feet and ran all the way back to the home of one of them where some of the disciples were gathered together, mourning the death of Jesus. "He is risen!" they exclaimed, shouting and crying all at once. "Angels were there amidst a great white Light and they told us that Jesus is alive!"

Of course, the disciples thought that the women had lost their senses and were hysterical from grief, and paid little attention to what they were saying. The men were rather annoyed at all the commotion, which interrupted their prayers. The women would not be silenced, however, and kept screaming that Jesus had left His tomb and was alive! When the men refused to listen, they ran outside to their neighbors to spread the news. There were a few whose hearts leapt with the anticipation of a great event and went with them, hoping they might see this miracle.

Meanwhile, a woman, one of the followers of Jesus, the Christ, had appeared near the tomb and was walking in one of the beautiful gardens that Joseph of Ramtha (Arimathea) had planted on his property. She was low in spirit, grieving that her Lord had been put to death and trying to understand what had happened and why. She came upon a gardener working in the soil who straightened as she came up the path and asked her why she looked so sad. She replied that her Lord had been crucified three days before and that her heart felt like it was dying, too. The gardener then called her by name and took her hand in His. She looked up into the face of Jesus, the Christ, and knew that He was not dead, but by her side, radiating a Light and Love she had never felt before, filling her being with an unbelievable joy! Suddenly, He was gone, leaving her with an everlasting peace that never again left her mind and inner being. She too went to tell the others, but at a slow pace that gave her time to live the experience over and over again in her mind.

The rest of the story is told quite well in your Bible, so I will not tell it again now. There is much more behind the Biblical story that should be told.

What happened to the body in the tomb? Did the tissue begin to disintegrate from the time the spirit left the body on the cross? Of course it did. That is the way of nature. In the heat of that climate, dead tissue begins to lose its texture very quickly and bodies were laid to rest immediately after death. Spices and salt were rubbed into the body, then it was wrapped in a long, white burial cloth. Instead of a casket, blocks of white stone upon which the body was laid were hewn and placed in the caves that served as tombs in that region. It was almost dark before the great round stone that served as a door to the tomb was finally rolled into place. Grooves had been chiseled into the side of the rock outside so that the stone would stay in place permanently. Inside, in the dark, the body of Jesus lay still and cold in the dank interior of the small cave.

The Resurrection

At midnight, a bright, white Light suddenly destroyed the darkness and filled every corner of the small room. A powerful Being of Light appeared in the midst of the piercing glare and began to emit strong high-vibrational beams to the still body. The wrappings fell away and the flesh of the body started to glow with a Light that began within it, and it took on a natural appearance. Then, the Great Being of Light moved to the body and slowly, as if dreading the idea, merged Itself with the body until they became one again. The body of Jesus, now completely the vessel of the Christ Spirit, rose to its feet. A robe of pure white appeared on the body and simple sandals were upon the feet. This body was not the same physical body made of matter that had been laid to rest in that place but was now a body of very high vibrations that could be manipulated by the Will of the Christ very easily. The Christ simply walked through the huge stone that stood in the entrance of the tomb and went on His way.

Within the great Light that remained in the tomb, angels appeared. It was they who caused the great stone to roll out of its place and fall back upon the ground.

Mankind was still in the darkness of little understanding. The resurrection of the body of Jesus by the Christ Spirit was not done to take away the sins of the world, as people have interpreted the miracle, but to teach mankind that a body composed of matter is but a tool to be used by the spirit of every created soul to experience the events which teach the important things each soul must learn. By entering the body once more, the Christ Spirit gave mankind the pattern of eternal life, the knowledge that the soul is eternal. He appeared to many people besides His disciples, so that there would be no question of who and what He was, no question that the rules of nature upon this planet had been overturned. There were many more who came to the knowledge of themselves and the Creator in those few days He walked the Earth in His glorified body.

When the time came to depart this part of the ancient world, the Christ traveled to all of the other then populated areas of the world to teach all people His Message of love. To think that the Creator of this world would only give of Himself to the inhabitants of one small nation is really quite arrogant. The intent of the Christ Spirit was to bring knowledge to all people and this was accomplished over a period of about one hundred of your years. When that was concluded to His satisfaction, the Christ Spirit, glorified body and all, rose back into the seventh dimension whence He had come.

The world had been given the Truth and it was now up to humanity to follow in the Path of Truth.

Question: I felt your thought about "the regions of death." The Apostles' Creed states, "He was crucified, died and was buried; He descended into hell; the third day He rose again from the dead; He ascended into heaven, and sitteth at the right hand of God the Father Almighty...." Would you explain "the regions of death"?

Thank you for the question. The interpretations of the original words written by the Apostles were rather spurious. The first interpreters were anxious to gain the attention of the masses along with the hierarchy of the church at that time, and they tried to set up conditions that would bind the masses to the church. The concept of hell was given to drive people to the arms of the church for protection, so to speak. The Creed you quote was written long centuries after the life of Jesus, the Christ, but the concept was still accepted. As you have seen from checking your Bible, there is no mention that Jesus, the Christ, ever descended anywhere, just that he died.

The "regions of death" that I referred to are the natural journeys of the soul from the third dimension, in which you now reside, through the regions where those of evil intent are kept until their enlightenment and upward into the fourth and higher dimensions. These words were given to the women to emphasize the importance of what had happened. The soul of Jesus, the man, took this path after his death and returned to the sixth dimension whence he had come. This soul is the being known as Sananda. His mission of incarnating into a body to be the vessel for the Christ Spirit was completed. When the Christ Spirit brought the body back to life in a higher vibration, He alone entered and occupied the body. Those of you who are seeking the truth will need to go back to the Bible. The truth is there; seek it out.

When you are downcast because of many problems, look into yourself and remember the great gift of love that has been given to you. It is always there, within you, to enfold you and give you strength. There is no greater love.

Given with love.

The Man Jesus

By Master Teacher Peter
1990

Master Peter: In the book *On Earth Assignment,* it is stated, "He could walk through solid matter, through molecular rearrangement. He could eat meat." Why was the eating of meat mentioned? Was it unusual because of his higher vibrations? Was he a meat-eater in the normal sense of the word? Did he eat pork or other meats that were forbidden by the Jews at the time and, if so, how did he deal with this?

Jesus was a man and, as such, needed the same foods as any other of his time. Because of the higher frequency of his body after the Christ Spirit entered it, it would have been impossible for his body to assimilate meat because of its heavy molecular structure had he not changed that structure when meat was being digested in his body. There were other substances, also hard even for the normal person to digest, that he had to take the same action for. He ate a lot of nuts, high-fiber grains and breads and so forth. The unwritten meaning in the book was to impress the fact that Jesus, the man, was also the Christ, Who had to make special concessions to the body He inhabited in order to maintain His spirit and body in a related manner.

There were many concessions the Christ Spirit had to make in order to inhabit a mortal body. He had to be aware of all of the bodily functions relating to the senses and cope with them as a human. He maintained the unconscious working of the body itself that he had been born into. The sexual urgings that came with the body He was able to sustain, as this is part of a male body that adds to its strength and vitality. As Jesus, the man, He knew well that by restraining the bodily use of the sex glands He would be able to have a much stronger spiritual energy to use for the work that was intended.

The body of Jesus was of a much higher vibration than has been supposed by humanity. True, after the death on the cross of the physical body, the Christ returned clothed in His etheric or spiritual body. However, merely the touch of Jesus, the man, was electrifying to all but the hardest-hearted of humans. Although not mentioned in the Bible (for fear of the truth's not being accepted), anyone who touched Jesus immediately received healing energy in one way or another, according to the need.

Jesus, the Christ, could have sustained the human body without having to eat material food, but He wanted to appear as normal as possible to those He was teaching and living with. They would have been afraid of Him at first had He not emulated the human beings He came to teach.

The Creator and Master of the Universe was not concerned about the opinions of little men who decided what their fellow men and women should eat, wear or do. He ate pork and even snake, if nothing else was available, to keep up His energy when necessary. He was considerate enough not to do so when in gatherings of people who did not believe this was the right thing to do, but He and His disciples ate what was available without restrictions. The priests were sometimes aware of this and spoke against Him in very colorful terms at times. This was one of the arguments they dared to bring up at His "trial." The eating of pork in those days was restricted for a very good reason, as you must well recognize. The presence of unseen worms or bacteria was not understood and illness easily resulted from consuming pork not completely cooked. Jesus was easily able to teach the importance of this to His disciples.

Given with love.

CHAPTER EIGHT

The "Second Coming"

By Master Teacher Peter
1990

Soon will come the day when all peoples of the Earth will see that the darkness in their hearts is caused by their own refusal to let the Light enter in. Jesus, the Christ, was portrayed in a painting with the figure of Jesus standing in a garden, knocking at a door that was symbolically the door of the heart. The artist would have been more accurate to have portrayed Jesus knocking from the inside of the heart, trying to persuade the owner to open his or her being to the Christ within.

The question among Christian people is, "When will the Christ come again?" The answer is, "He never left!"

The Bible says that the Christ will come again in like manner as He left. This gives the impression that the Christ will appear in a mass of clouds and descend from the heavens. This also assumes that the Christ has been living unseen in a heaven beyond our senses and sight. This is true to an extent. However, the Great soul that is the Christ lives within each one of us (yes, in all of us in the spiritual world, too) and, at the same time, He is actively creating and directing the events that keep our universe in constant balance.

He has appeared many times to incarnated beings on Planet Earth since His resurrection. You have books now that tell of His visits to many primitive peoples at that time, and they are essentially correct. Why does

197

one group of people always think no one else is entitled to heavenly visitations? During the centuries, the Master has appeared and still does appear to many people in dreams and visions for different reasons. It is rare that a soul entity who is diligently on the path has not had at least one vision or dream of the Christ. This is His way of touching and giving encouragement to the student, as every good teacher will do.

Look around and observe the many times you see another person imitate, during some event in his or her life, an action simulating or relating to flying. In dreams most people find themselves flying above the ground, feeling very natural doing so. The act of flying has always been depicted in paintings of religious subjects as a celestial or very spiritual person leaving the Earth and either flying or levitating. Flying is universal symbolism for the releasing of the spirit from the body, either to travel separately during the sleep process or to return to the spiritual kingdom whence it came. When people experience a spiritual "high," they feel light and want to be higher from the ground than they are. This is where the term "getting high" originated.

The vault of heaven has always been the place to reach up to when there is a feeling of intense delight or joy, and especially while having a beautiful spiritual experience. It is the natural direction one's inner being wishes to go — back to Spirit.

No wonder, then, that the human family looks to the heavens in expectation of seeing a huge figure of the Christ displayed across the sky in an intense white Light, accompanied by legions of angels playing horns! It is natural to look up and expect to see wondrous things. Perhaps the Christ will oblige his children and give them such a display.

The good news is that there is no waiting for the main event. It is happening now. Although an essence of the Christ Spirit is born into every soul entity incarnating into human life, the intensity of the presence has been and is increasing every day. The heavy energies that are coming into the world now are part of the Second Coming of the Christ. The energy itself is part of the power of the Christ. The energy you feel sometimes that comes without warning and even makes you feel dizzy for a while is part of the Christ Spirit announcing His increased presence. He is here now!

The Beast in the Book of the Revelation is making himself known in the Middle East during the continuing wars in this region. Soon you will start to hear rumors about a man who is trying to bring the Arab nations together to avoid another war and perhaps a global conflict. He will be a statesman who, although a young man, has great powers as a mediator and attracts followers wherever he goes. Watch and listen, but do not fall under his spell.

The Christ Spirit is also waiting and watching while the power of the Beast's influence is rapidly making itself known. The Christ will not interfere with the wars nor with the Beast. Prophecy must work itself out and mankind will have to deal with it.

It is up to humanity to watch for the coming within themselves. How can one acknowledge the Christ Spirit if the mind is too loaded with ideas from many different sources and/or religions? Inner confusion does not lend itself to clarity of belief or purpose. It is better to keep the mind open and clear so that when the truth is heard, from any source, it will be recognized from deep within.

There are many today who want to be leaders of groups of people and teach them whatever they think people want to hear, because that will bind a group to a leader. Beware of such material. The truth is not always what you want to hear and may be far beyond what you are able to understand. Even so, if you are truly able to let your inner voice tell you of its validity, accept it and learn all you can about it. Stretch your mind; give yourself time to think about the material and let it turn your present thinking around, if need be. Work with it in your life and see the difference it can make, and it will. Read the Bible again and see how the truth makes the old words come alive and sound more meaningful. Sometimes religion has given and is continuing to give the holy words meanings different from what they were intended to convey. Read as if you had never read them before and pure understanding will flood your mind.

There is still a long time to come before the Christ Spirit will take over a world cleansed of the dark forces. It is a time to look forward to, indeed, but right now it is important that the Christ within be recognized and accepted. The intensity of His presence is becoming more evident every day. Instead of fighting the inner pressures, give yourself times when you can still the mind to listen and feel that presence. The greatest friend you will ever have is waiting there for you. Follow His ways and the path will become shorter and wider; knowledge and love will make your way easier and more fulfilling.

He is knocking within your heart, patiently waiting to be acknowledged and heard. Open the door.

Given with love.

SUGGESTED READING

The books listed below have given me the most meaningful information and inspiration during my journey along the Path. There are many, many others, of
course. Let your inner feelings direct you to the
book that your spiritual counselors know is best for
you at any given time.
God bless you in your quest for knowledge.
Ruth Ryden

The Holy Bible

EDGAR CAYCE – The Association for Research and Enlightenment
(A.R.E.), an organization formed to bring the information he
brought forth from the infinite into written form, has published
many, many books of his writings. The book, *There is a River*, by
Thomas Sugrue is the story of Mr. Cayce's life and is a very powerful introduction to the way God sends information to humanity in
these times. Many people have found their awakening in these
pages.

Many Mansions by Gina Cerminara. This is an excellent introduction to
reincarnation.

SETH is a being channeled by Jane Roberts in a number of books.
I feel they are important because of the many different concepts
presented for our understanding. The books may be a bit advanced, but they are worthwhile if taken a little at a time.

*The Starseed Transmissions; Vision; Terra Christa; Starseed – The Third
Millennium.* These four books are all by Ken Carey and should be
read in this order. These are the most beautiful books of channeled
material I have ever read. Even for the beginner, there is a world of
understanding here.